Agriculture in Iraq:
Resources, Potentials, Constraints, and Research Needs and Priorities

Executive Summary 5

1. Introduction 8

2. Regional Patterns: 10
    2.1. Climate 10
    2.2. Physiography 14
    2.3. Population...21

3. Land and Water Resources 24
    3.1. Land resources 24
    3.2. Land Use 24
    3.3. Land Degradation 25
    3.4. River Basins 26
    3.5. Surface Water Resources 26
    3.6. Ground Water Resources 28
    3.7. Dams 28
    3.8. New Watercources 28
    3.9. Water Withdrawal 29
    3.10. Irrigation and Drainage 29
    3.11. Irrigated Areas 29
    3.12. Salinity 30
    3.13. Trends in Water Resources Management 32

4. Soils of Iraq 35

5. The Agrarian Structure 37
    5.1. Institutional Environment 37
    5.2. Land reform 37

6. Biodiversity and Plant Genetic Resources 40
    6.1. Biodiversity 40
    6.2. Plant Genetic resources 41

7. Crops 44
    7.1 Small Grains 45
    7.2 .Food Legumes 47
    7.3. Industrial Crops 48
    7.4. Vegetables 48
    7.5. Fruit Trees 49
    7.6. Date Palm 50
    7.7. Medicinal Plants 52

7.8. Crop Protection 53
7.9. Seed Industry 54

8. Forest Resources 56
    8.1. Natural Forests 56
    8.2. Afforestation and Reforestation 57
    8.3. Fuelwood and Wood Products Needs 58

9. Rangelands 60
    9.1. Rangeland Management and Rehabilitation 60
    9.2. Rangelands Problems 61
    9.3. Alternative Feed Sources 63

10. Livestock 65
    10.1. Livestock Production and Management 65
    10.2. Animal Health 66

11. Fisheries and Aquaculture 68

12. Apiculture 70

13. The National Agricultural Research System (NARS) of Iraq 71
    13.1. Historical background 71
    13.2. The current NARS 72
    13.3. Research Policy 74
    13.4. Human Resources 76
    13.5. Financial and Physical Resources 76
    13.6. National and International Linkages 77

14. Research Needs and Priorities 78
    14.1. Restructuring the National Agricultural Research System 78
    14.2. Capacity Building 78
    14.3. Strengthening the Role of Iraqi Universities in Ag. Research 79
    14.4. Research Needs and Priorities in the Rainfed, Irrigated and
        Rangeland Production Systems of Iraq. 81
15. Selected References. 83

Executive Summary

Since the early 1980s, it has been extremely difficult to obtain accurate statistics and reliable information on agricultural activities within Iraq. During the last two decades, agricultural systems in the dry-, irrigated- and range-lands of that country faced an unprecedented pressure to meet the food requirements of a population increasing at about 3% annually. The current situation is creating new, more intensive, and more diverse demands on farmers, agricultural producers and planners. Although the agricultural sector, during the last decade, has been given high priority to ensure food security through greater self-sufficiency, the country, and for the foreseeable future, will continue to depend on imported food.

During the last 2 decades, Iraqi agriculture faced increasing pressure to feed a population of 22.8 m, increasing at a 3.6% rate annually.

The agrarian sector in Iraq witnessed a number of drastic measures during the last 40 years. These include: land reform, cooperative and collective state farming, central planning and, finally, private ownership. Estimates of cultivable land areas vary from 5-8 million ha; however, no more than 3.5 million ha (47% irrigated and 53% dryland farming) have been actually cultivated.

Rural to urban migration within the country is widespread, and threatens the social and economic stability. The demographic pressure on the land combined with the need to produce more food from a limited, and shrinking, resource base of land and water are forcing farmers to follow exploitative production practices that maximize short-term returns at the expense of long-term sustainability.

Iraq has ~ 11.0 m ha of arable land; 3.5 m ha are cultivated.

Decreasing water resources may force a structural adjustment of the agricultural sector.

Renewable fresh water resources are estimated at about 2,000 m^3/person/year; however, Iraq faces huge water problems; these are caused by geographic, topographic and management factors. Major structural adjustments in the agricultural sector are needed to solve water management problems in the country.

Growing water shortages, especially from the Euphrates, were characteristic of the 1990s. With continued population growth, irrigated agriculture has to compete with the municipal and industrial sectors for water. The combined Iraqi water demand on the Tigris and Euphrates in the period after 2020 would range from 70,000 to 90,000 MCM. This could result in a negative balance of 15,000 MCM, mainly on the Euphrates. Just how severely this water shortage will impact Iraq's agriculture is impossible to estimate at the present time.

Prior to 1990, Iraq produced about one-third of its annual basic food needs and spent about US$ 2 billion to import the balance of its requirements. Since then, despite emphasis on increasing food production, and despite the Oil-for-Food Program, undertaken under the auspices of the United Nations since1996, the country continues to face deterioration in the agricultural sector.

Agricultural production remains constrained due to lack of quality seed, herbicides, insecticides, fertilizers, animal vaccines, machinery, irrigation equipment and spare parts. Moreover, water resources in the drylands are declining (estimated at 43% of normal levels in 1998) due to a severe drought which devastated crops on ~70% of the rainfed arable land in the country. It is estimated that Iraq will need US$ 3.5 billion to import basic foods to meet the annual shortages during the next decade.

Farmers in Iraq are struggling to produce under poor environmental conditions with few tools for coping with drought, salinity, pests, and shortages of inputs and lack of appropriate technologies. Iraqi cereal production dropped sharply in the past decade due to problems with its seed multiplication system, leading to degradation of seed quality and productivity. Planting low-quality seeds during the 1980s and 1990s led to problems of weed infestation and pest attacks, low productivity and an inability to use seed-processing machinery efficiently. Lack of high-yielding seed has reduced farm efficiency and often forced poor farmers to abandon their lands.

Iraqi farmers have to cope with drought, salinity, pests, lack of inputs and lack of appropriate technologies.

Land degradation, salinization, and declining crop yields due to mismanagement of land resources and lack of inputs, are serious problem, especially in the irrigated lands. The country's rangelands and forest resources are deteriorating mainly as a result of overstocking what are essentially fragile ecosystems and because of deforestation for fuelwood and charcoal.

The livestock sector experienced serious problems during the last decade because of shortages of feed, veterinary services and vaccines. Number of farm animals declined during the last decade, and in spite of the government's efforts to boost livestock production, meat and milk production declined by 24% during the late 1980s as compared to the 1970s.

Performance of the agricultural sector in Iraq during the last two decades was disappointing, not only as a result of environmental constraints (e.g., drought) but also due to poor management and inadequate planning and allocation of trained human resources; agricultural extension services and agricultural vocational education, in particular, are in need of major improvements.

Iraq faces serious problems of environmental degradation that must be addressed immediately because failure to act now will greatly compound the cost and complexity of later remedial efforts, and because environmental degradation is beginning to pose a major threat to human well-being, especially among the poor.

To deal with the multiple challenges imposed upon it by internal and external factors, the agricultural sector in Iraq has to structurally adjust itself to address socio-economic, land-use, livestock production and feed resources, water resources, agro-ecology, environmental protection, and research and extension components in a holistic, multidisciplinary and long-term manner.

Environmental degradation in the agricultural sector is a serious problem.

1. Introduction

Mesopotamia, the ancient land of the "twin rivers" (the Tigris and Euphrates), with its bountiful land, fresh waters, and varying climates, contributed to the human civilization in many ways. The eastern limb of the Fertile Crescent was the cradle of the earliest known civilizations and served as the cultural heart from which the first ideas of sedentary agriculture, domestication of animals, the wheel, writing, and urban development are believed to have diffused westward to the Nile Valley and eastward to the Indus Valley.

Since the beginning of recorded time, agriculture has been the primary economic activity of the people of old Mesopotamia and modern-day Iraq. Agriculture was the country's major economic activity in the 1920s; however, its contribution to the gross domestic product (GDP) dropped to 42% in 1981 and 18% in 1990. Even so, 13% of the labor force continues to be engaged in agriculture, more than in any other sector except services.

The land area of Iraq is 438,317 km^2, with a population of 22.8 m and a population density of 52 per km^2. Arable land as percentage of total land is relatively small (12%) and agriculture, in 2001, contributed 6.1% to the GDP. More than half (53%) of the arable land is rainfed, nearly all of it in the northern uplands; however, most of the agricultural production comes from the more intensively cultivated areas of the irrigated plains.

Agriculture has been the primary economic activity in Iraq for millennia. Now, it contributes only 6% of GDP and employs 13% of labor force.

In the decade from 1977, Iraq was self sufficient in cereals, and agricultural imports amounted to 22% of total imports. During recent decades, however, Iraq has shifted from net food exporter to food importer. This shift was prompted by several factors, including population increase, a rising standard of living, increased industrialization, migration of farm workers to urban centers, and loss of soil productivity in poorly drained irrigated areas of the south.

Increased funding for agricultural research is particularly critical in Iraq. Despite this nation's heavy dependence on agriculture, the public expenditures on research generally total less than 0.5 percent of its agricultural gross domestic product. By comparison, industrialized countries spend 2 to 5 percent.

Prior to 1990, Iraq had one of the highest per capita food availability in the Middle East, because of its relative prosperity and capacity to import large quantities of food, which met up to two-thirds of food requirements. After 1990, however, Iraq's ability to import food was significantly constrained.

Agricultural development will be a great challenge over the next two decades in Iraq. Food requirements will double as the population continues to grow at 3.0% annually. There is an estimated 8m ha of cultivable land, but only 4-5 million ha is cultivated in any one year, and the land area under high-value vegetables and fruits is relatively very small (< 0.5 million ha). In order to achieve self sufficiency in cereals, Iraq has to grow wheat and barley on 8.1 million ha.

Iraq is a net food importer. Agricultural imports make up 22% of all imports. Iraq will spend US$ 3.0 billion/year on food imports in years to come.

The role of women in agriculture, especially in the production process and extension, needs to be addressed, as more and more women are involved in food production, processing and marketing.

This paper presents overviews of agricultural resources and institutional constraints on agriculture in Iraq; and outlines research needs and priorities for this important sector of the Iraqi economy.

2. Regional Patterns

Iraq lies between 29°15'N, and 38°15'N, 38°45 and 48°45'E, and is located entirely within the north temperate zone where it enjoys stimulus seasonality of climate. Iraq, with a total area of 438,320 km² including 924 km² of inland waters, is surrounded by Iran to the east, Turkey to the north, Syria and Jordan to the west, Saudi Arabia and Kuwait to the south, and the Persian Gulf to the southeast. Topographically, Iraq is shaped like a basin, consisting of the Great Mesopotamian alluvial plain of the Tigris and Euphrates. This plain is surrounded by mountains in the north and the east, which can reach altitudes of 3,550 m above sea level, and by desert areas in the south and west, which account for over 40% of the land area. For administrative purposes, the country is divided into 18 governorates, three of which are included in the northern autonomous region.

> *Iraq's land area is 438,320 km², including 924 km² of inland waters.*
>
> *The great alluvial Mesopotamian Plain is the main agricultural producing region.*

2.1. Climate

The climate of Iraq is mainly of the continental, subtropical semi-arid type, with the north and northeastern mountainous regions having a Mediterranean climate. Rainfall occurs during the winter months, from December to February in most parts of the country and November to April in the mountains, with average day temperature of 16°C dropping at night to 2°C with a possibility of frost. Summers are dry and hot to extremely hot, with a shade temperature of over 43°C during July and August, yet dropping at night to 26°C. Rainfall is highly erratic in time, quantity and locations, and ranges from less than 100mm in the south and southwest to about 1,000 mm/year in the north and northeast. The substantial variation in amount and distribution of rainfall increases the risk to rainfed crop production.

Roughly 90% of the annual rainfall occurs between November and April, most of it in the winter months from December through March. The remaining six months, particularly the hottest ones of June, July, and August, are dry.

Except in the north and northeast, mean annual rainfall ranges between 100 and 170 mm. Data available from stations in the foothills and steppes south and southwest of the mountains indicate that mean annual rainfall ranges between 350 and 600 mm for that area. Annual rainfall in the mountains is more abundant and may reach 1000 mm in some locations, however, the terrain precludes extensive cultivation. Cultivation on non-irrigated land is limited essentially to the mountain valleys, foothills, and steppes, which may receive 300 mm of annual rainfall. Even in this zone only one crop a year can be grown, and shortages of rain have often led to crop failures.

Average precipitation for the whole country (1961-1990) was 216 mm/year or 94.7 km^3/year. Total internal renewable water resources amounted to 35.3 km^3/year during the same period. Agricultural water use was 92% of all water resources or 39.38 km^3/year.

Mean minimum temperatures in the winter range from near freezing (just before dawn) in the northern and northeastern foothills and the western desert to 2-5°C in the alluvial plains of southern Iraq. Temperatures rise to a mean maximum of about 15.5°C in the western desert and the northeast, and 16.6°C in the south. During summer, mean minimum temperatures range from about 22.2°C to about 29°C and rise to maximums roughly between 37.7 and 43.3°C. Temperatures sometimes fall below freezing, and as low as -14.4°C at Rutbah in the western desert. Maximum temperatures are more likely to reach 46°C in the summer months, and several stations have records of over 48°C.

The climate varies from Mediterranean to continental & sub-tropical, semi-arid type.

Rainfall varies from <100 mm in the south to >1,000 mm in the northeast.

Temperature drops to below zero °C in the north and reaches ~ 50°C in the south

The summer months are marked by two kinds of wind phenomena. The southern and southeasterly *Sharqi*, a dry, dusty wind with occasional gusts of eighty kilometers an hour, occurs from April to early June and again from late September through November. It may last for a day at the beginning and end of the season but for several days at other times. This wind is often accompanied by violent dust storms that may rise to heights of several thousand meters and close airports for brief periods. From mid-June to mid-September the prevailing wind, called the *Shamal*, is from the north and northwest. It is a steady wind, absent only occasionally during this period. The very dry air brought by this *Shamal* permits intensive sun heating of the land surface, but the breeze has some cooling effect.

The combination of rain shortages and extreme heat makes much of Iraq a desert. Because of very high rates of evaporation, soil and plants rapidly lose the little moisture obtained from the rain, and vegetation may not survive without extensive irrigation. Some areas, however, although arid, do have natural vegetation in contrast to the desert. For example, in the Zagros Mountains in northeastern Iraq there is permanent vegetation, such as oak trees, and date palms are found in the south.

In winter, this inflow is frequently interrupted by cyclonic activities, a part of the irregular westerly circulation of middle latitudes which penetrates deep in the southern parts of the country. The yearly average number of these east-moving cyclones amounts to 120. Most precipitation is associated with these weak cyclones.

Occasionally, a well-developed cyclone may remain stagnant over the country for several days. This draws in large bodies of maritime air, associated with considerable amounts of rain in the lowlands, and heavy snowfall in the mountains. In general, there is a gradual increase in rainfall in a north-east direction, from 50mm in the south-western corner to about 1000 mm in the high mountainous area of the northeast. Precipitation in the mountains is influenced by a combination of cyclonic activity and orographic barriers. The 200 mm isohyet, in general, indicates the southern limits of the rain-fed agricultural zone. Large daily and annual temperature amplitudes are pronounced continental climatic characteristic. Annual average temperature in Baghdad is 22.5°C and mean daily minimum temperature in January is 4°C. Mean maximum temperature in August is 43.2°C. Air humidity is rather low; in Baghdad, the relative humidity in August ranges from 20 to 45 percent.

The climate of Iraq, in terms of temperature and rainfalls, may be classified into three main types.

2.1.1. Mediterranean Climate

This type is characterized by cool wet winters and hot dry summers. It is more restricted to the mountainous areas; therefore, snowfall is not uncommon and the amount of rainfall varies from 400mm at lower altitudes to 1,000mm at higher altitudes. Average summer temperature do not exceed 35° C on the lower slopes, but it is much less on higher slopes.

2.1.2. Steppe Climate

This type is transitional one between the Mediterranean type in the north and the desert in the south. High temperature and small amounts of rain are the main limiting factors. Annual rainfall ranges from 200mm to 400mm. It comes during the cool season of the year when the evaporation rate is the lowest. This is a natural pasture area; large sheep flocks are grazed during late winter to mid summer time.

2.1.3. Hot Desert Climate

The climate of the lowlands of Iraq is a typical desert climate. This is an area of a high thermal energy. With clear sky during summer, air temperature rises to a maximum of 45-50° C. with a wide range

13

in daily temperature. Nights are rather cool. In winter times, warm and sunny weather prevails, and the temperature rarely drops below freezing point.

2.2. Physiography

Mountains, plateaus, hills and valleys, planes and inland water-covered areas are the major geomorphic forms, which, in varying combinations, constitute the topography of Iraq. These geomorphic forms exert a strong influence upon the cultural and economic patterns of the country and, together with the climate, provide a permanent back-drop against which the history of Iraq is enacted.

A mountain movement started 50 to 30 million years ago, and a series of sedimentary beds, lying at the bottom of the shallow sea, has been regularly bent into arches and troughs; that is, into anticlines and synclines. The arches formed the mountains and troughs formed the valleys. The mountain building movement is still going on, but at a very slow rate. During the three main pluvial periods in Iraq, concurrent with glacial ages in Europe, climate was more humid than at present and a considerable period of river erosion modified the land surface. The mountains were cut down and the valleys as well as the southern part of the extensive geosynclines were filled up with pebbles, gravel, sand, silt and clay. Inter-pluvial phases, with a climate similar to that of the present time, interrupted the erosional process, and river terraces have been formed along the rivers and their tributaries in central and northern Iraq. Three broad erosional river terraces, for example, can be seen in Tikrit along the eastern banks of the Tigris.

Four broad altitudinal topographic regions can be distinguished in Iraq. These are:

2.2.1. Mountain Region

Bold, majestic mountains cover an area of 92,000 km^2, or about 21 percent, of the total area. The mountain region extends mainly in the northern and north-eastern parts of the country. The mountains consist mainly of parallel anticline ridges separated by elongated synclinal valleys. But they are united by narrow gorges, the outlets of the drainage of the interior basins. The mountains, for the greater part, are eroded and the detritus material has been deposited in the valleys and in the area in front of the mountains. The mountains are comprised of various folded limestone layers varying from simple folding in the south to complicated folding in

the north. Sindy, Zab and Rawandooz geosynclines separate these two parts. The average elevation of the former, ranges from 1,700 to 2,000 meters, while it reaches an elevation of 2,300 to 3,000 meters in the latter. Faults, metamorphic rocks, and glacial landforms are not uncommon in this area. The highest mountain peak in the country is Hassarrost; it stands 3,607 meters above sea level.

Northern mountains make up 21% of land area. Highest peak is 3,607 m.

Mostly covered with forest trees and grazing grounds

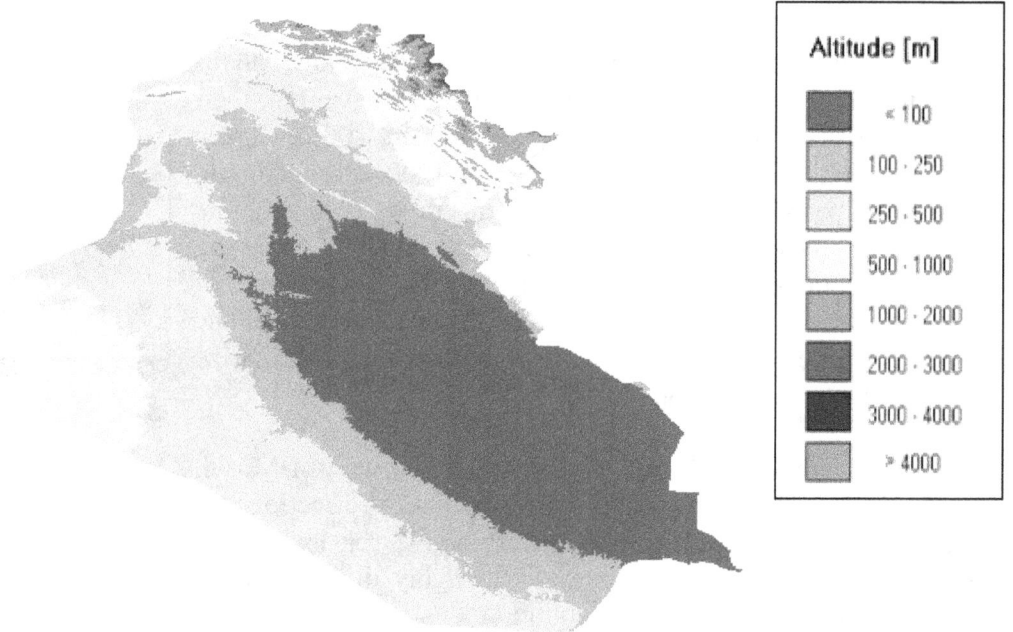

Altitude [m]

■	« 100
▨	100 - 250
☐	250 - 500
☐	500 - 1000
▨	1000 - 2000
■	2000 - 3000
■	3000 - 4000
▨	» 4000

Fig. 2. Land forms in Iraq.

Uplands, piedmont, and rugged mountains rising northeast of the upper Tigris in Iraq exhibit a sharp contrast to the desert plains areas that cover most of the rest of the country.

The highest ridges contain Iraq's only forests, some of them quite extensive, preserved by the isolation and ruggedness of the area. Most of the mountain slopes permit only grazing, lower and more gentile slopes support fruit and nut trees, and the broad valley bottoms are intensively cultivated.

Water-falls, cascades, rapids and deep gorges are common geomorphic phenomena in the area. Plains of a considerable size, such as Rania and Shahrazoor, separate two mountain areas. The former is a kidney-shaped plain, in the Lesser Zab area, with an elevation ranging from 500 to 700 meters. It extends for 30 km and its width varies from 20 to 30 km. A basin-like Shahrazoor plain varies in elevation from 400 to 700 meters above sea level and extends for 45 km from east to west, while its narrowest width is about 50 km.

2.2.2. Undulating Lands

This area is comprised of a fairly hilly landscape, located south and west of the mountain region. It covers an area of about 42,000 km^2, or nearly 9.6% of Iraq's total area. Although there are some similarities with the former region, general landscape differences stand sharp. The area is somewhat folded in the later phase of folding. It consists of low parallel hill ridges, wide shallow valleys and extensive plains, in which various streams have cut their valleys. In general, average altitude varies from 200 to 1,000 meters. Local relief ranges from a minimum of 200 to a maximum of 800 meters per square kilometer. Beds of gravel, conglomerate and sandstone make up the area. It can be divided, in terms of geomorphic landforms structure, surface rocks and degree of erosional process, into a number of plains, plateaus, mountains and hill ridges. A briefly discussed example of each may summarize the whole picture of the region.

The undulating lands cover 9.6% of Iraq. They make up the major rainfed agricultural area.

The mountains are relatively low. Sinjar mountain, west of Mosul, is an anticline range extending in a north-easterly direction. Its elevation varies from 900 to 1600 meters above sea level. The southern edge of the mountain range is a highly dissected part. Strike valleys and minor scraps are common.

Plateaus are small in number, and the best known are those of Mosul and Kirkuk. The surface of Mosul plateau is dissected by shallow valleys with hills rising to 400 meters above the surrounding valley bottoms.

Plains are found within the area such as the plains of Sinjar and Arbil. The latter is a synclinal triangular basin filled with alluvium deposits. Its elevation varies from about 600 m at the eastern edge to 350 m at the western parts. Fertile soils together with an adequate amount of winter rain provide a good basis for agricultural land use. Wheat and barely are the main crops in winter, while underground water resources supply enough irrigation water for many agricultural crops during summer.

Crops such as wheat, barley, sugar beet, cotton, vegetables, and fruits, dairy products, and agricultural industries (e.g., sugar, cotton, woolen textiles, etc.) form the basis of a solid agricultural economy. During winter, a significant growth of annual grasses and legumes, depending on rainfall, provides good natural pasture for sheep, goats and cattle.

2.2.3. The Depositional Plain

The cultural and economic core of ancient and modern-day Iraq evolved in the southern Mesopotamian alluvial plains, along and between the lower courses of the Tigris and Euphrates. Ancient empires thrived, and the ruins of most ancient cities of the Old World still stand in this part of the country.

Temperatures during the dry summers average 35°C for July and soar to daytime highs of 50°C. The plains drop from 80 m above sea level near Baghdad to sea level near Basra in the south.

The Mesopotamian plain is the cultural and economic core of ancient and modern-day Iraq. It covers 30% of the land area and produces most of its crops under irrigation.

Southeast of the Baghdad area, the central interfluve is mostly wasteland or marshes that become desiccated in the dry, hot summers. A high water table and inadequate drainage on some of these deltaic silt lands combine to raise soil salinity to levels that prevent cultivation of otherwise fertile soils that could be irrigated if adequate drainage could be maintained.

It is the plain of the twin rivers, the Tigris and the Euphrates, referred to in ancient times as *Shinar* and later on called *Al-Sawad* (i.e., black lands), because of its high agricultural productivity. The plain is located in central and southern Iraq with a number of distinct landscapes. The undulating lands are to the north, the western plateau to the west, Zagros mountains to the east and the Persian Gulf to the south. The plains (including marshland and lakes) cover an area of 132,500 km^2, or 30.2% of the total area of Iraq. It has a northwest-southeast orientation, trending in the same direction of the Tigris, Euphrates and *Shatt al-Arab*.

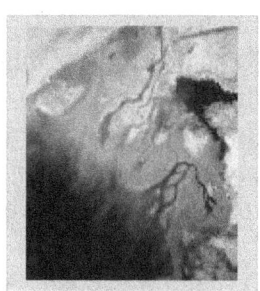

Most of the uplands, extending from Syria into central Iraq, are a desert plateau descending from 450 m in the northeast to 80 m near Baghdad. Except for the river floodplains and for the segment northwest of Mosul, population is sparse and development relatively limited. The undulating plateau in the north is devoted to rainfed cultivation of wheat and barley. Iraqi development plans envision later development of this part of the country, including appreciable irrigation, comparable to that undertaken by Syria.

Geologically, the plain occupies the southern part of an extensive geosyncline. It was filled up during the quaternary and recent geological periods. Besides sediments carried by the twin rivers, some material of aeolian origin, blown out of the desert, is accumulated and mixed with fluvial deposits. As a result of flood and irrigation, rather thick layers of mud have been deposited on top of the original soils. Nearly the whole plain is now covered by this silty material.

Along the eastern borders, rivers tumbling down from the eastern mountains helped to form a number of alluvial fans. A series of adjacent fans coalesced to form an extensive piedmont alluvial plain. The material comprising these fans varies in texture, from coarse boulders and pebbles at its head to fine material down its slope. Mendile and Basra are located on such alluvial fans. Here is a good example of a successful agricultural land use. Gentle slopes, fertile loamy soils, good air drainage in winter and flow irrigation were utilized to grow date palms and citrus fruits.

Most of the plain appears to be dead flat. In areas away from rivers or cultivated land, one may look to the full circle of the horizon without seeing any perceptible slope. But natural levees, irrigation canals, and low lying hills may break the monotony of the land.

Rivers flow with a gentle gradient and are unable to carry all their load of sediment. For this reason, natural levees capped with dikes border the Tigris and Euphrates. Flow irrigation canals can be easily led away from the rivers. Many parts of the plain have poor drainage, especially in the basin-like area in its southern part north of Basra.

Marshlands used to occupy an area of more than 35,000 km². Their geographic distribution may be seen in three distinct groups. The first stretches east and west of the Tigris, the second is Al-Hammar lake, and the third stretches between the Hilla canal and the Euphrates.

Reeds and bushes thickly cover the banks and shallow portions of the marshes. These provide an excellent nestling grounds for migrating birds in winter. The main crops grown on the marsh borders are rice, millet and tomatoes, while animal husbandry is restricted to raising buffaloes.

A natural wetland vegetation typically covered the bulk of the marshes. Common reed (*Phragmaites communis*) dominated the core of the permanent marshes, gradually yielding to reed mace (*Typha augustata*) in the ephemeral seasonal zone. Temporarily inundated mudflats are overgrown with salt-tolerant vegetation of low sedges and bulrush (*Carex* and *Juncus* spp., *Scripus brachyceras*). Deeper, permanent lakes support rich submerged aquatic vegetation typified by species such as hornwort

The marshes, a unique ecosystem, covered ~ 35,000 km² in southern Iraq before they were drained in the late 1990s.

(*Ceratophyllum demersum*) eel grass (*Vallisneria* spp.) and pondweed (*Potamogeton lucens*), as well as bottom vegetation such as stonewart (*Chara* spp.). In the smaller lakes and back swamps, floating vegetation of water lilies (*Nymphaea* and *Nuphar* spp.), water soldier (*Pistia stratiotes*) and duck weed (*Lemna gibba*) are common.

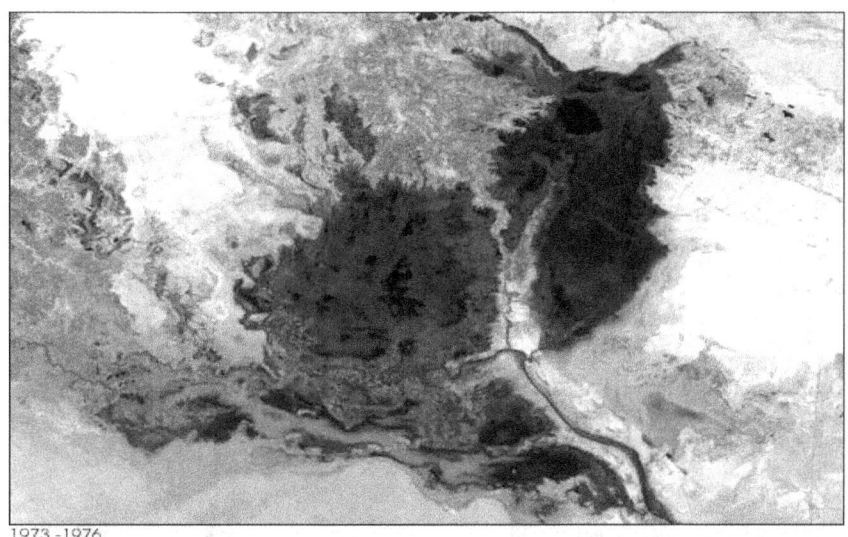

1973 -1976

2000

Fig. 3. Marshlands in Iraq before (upper) and after (below) they were drained.

As a major haven of regional and global biodiversity, the marshlands support significant populations and species of wildlife. Recently, however, and after large parts of the marshes were drained, the number of endangered species of birds, mammals and fish were estimated at 11, 5, and 1, respectively.

19

2.2.4. The Western Plateau (Semi-desert)

This extension of the Syrian and Arabian deserts lies west of the Euphrates Valley and comprises the barren western third of Iraq. It is the realm of Iraq's few thousand remaining Bedouins and least populated and least developed part of the country.

This is the largest physiographic region in the country. It occupies an area of 171,817 km^2, or about 39.2% of Iraq's total area. The surface rises gradually from 120 m in the east to 700 m in the west. Surface drainage takes a general west-east direction, but streams bring large amounts of water from Sinjar mountain to be drained southward to the Wadi Tharthar, which has been used to store excess Tigris water diverted near the Samarra Barrage. It was lately connected with the Euphrates and the Tigris by two feeding canals to divert enough irrigation water back to both rivers.

> *The western plateau is desert, semi-desert, and natural grazing grounds. It occupies 39.2% of the land area.*

Within this very extensive region, there are a number of different plains; *Al-Widian* (valleys), *Jezira* (island), *al-Hijara* (rock), *al-Hamad* and *Dibdibba*. The differences are based on physical factors such as relief and rock formations.

Al-Widian Plain developed in an area of limestone and gypsum rock ranging from level to undulating with shallow to rather deep valleys. In the northern Widian area is the large Ga'ara depression north of Rutba.

The Jezira is what has remained of an old inland sea. It is a dissected up land area across which the rivers flow in a well-developed valley. At present it is a large desert and steppe area. In winter and spring, especially after a good rainy season, the northern portion is covered by desert grasses which provide grazing grounds for camels and sheep. There are many saline lakes, marshes and depressions in this region, with Wadi Tharthar as the largest one.

Al-Hijara is a flat, stony plain with some shallow valleys. Al-Hamad plain is at the extreme western corner of the country. It developed on limestone bedrock formations. The plain is nearly level and featureless. Dibdibba plain occupies the southern portion of this region west of Basra. It developed on sand and gravel and the surface varies from level to slightly rolling land

Landforms of wrappings, foldings and faults are found throughout the region. Al-Ga'ara and Al-Salman basins occupy eroded domes, while geomorphic arid landforms are found in many localities.

Buttes and mesas are characteristics of isolated remnants of hard resistant limestone. Sand dunes 30 meters high, as well as low volcanic ones, are typical desert features.

2.3. Population

Iraq's estimated population of 22.8m, of which 25% is rural, in 2001 marked a 360 percent increase over 1947. This growth has occurred primarily through natural increase. Iraq's population is concentrated in linear patterns along the banks of rivers and canals on the plains but is more generally distributed in the villages and towns of the northeastern uplands and mountains. Average population density is estimated at 47 inhabitants/km^2, but ranges from 5 inhabitants/km^2 in the western (desert) part of the country, to more than 170 inhabitants/km² in the Babylon province, in the centre of the country. Population density is expected to reach 97 inhabitants/km^2 by the year 2025.

The average population growth was estimated at 3.6% during 1980-90, but emigration of foreign workers and severe economic hardships have reduced this growth rate since 1990. In 1989, the agriculture sector contributed only 5% to GDP, which was dominated by oil (61%). About 20% of the labor force is engaged in agriculture

Iraq's population is 22.8 m and growing at 3.6% per year. Rural population ~ 25%.

Population density ranges fro 5 to 170 person/ km2. It will double in the next 20 years.

The greatest single concentration of population, about 50% of the total, begins north and west of Baghdad, sprawls westward and southward across the mid-Iraq interfluve, and then follows the Euphrates and its various branches along the west side of the alluvial plain to the city of Samawah. Metropolitan Baghdad alone has one-third of Iraq's population. The middle Euphrates concentration has a well-balanced economy, based on agriculture, industry, trade, and tourism.

Secondary concentrations of population are found in the south, normally along Shat Al-Arab, with Basra as its largest city; in the north around Mosul; and in the northeast piedmont, around the oil developments in Kirkuk and the ancient city of Arbil. The remaining parts of the country are comparatively sparsely populated, with some 75% of the population living in urban centers.

21

Fig. 4. Population density in Iraq.

2.3.1. Settlement Patterns

In the rural areas of the alluvial plain and in the lower Diyala region, settlements almost invariably cluster near the rivers, streams, and irrigation canals; the levees, laid down by streams and canals, proved to be advantageous for both settlements and agriculture. Surface water drains more easily on the levees' backslope, and the coarse soils of the levees are easier to cultivate and permit better subsurface drainage. The height of the levees gives some protection against floods and the frost that often affect low-lying areas and may kill winter crops. Above all, those living or cultivating on the crest of a levee have easy access to water for irrigation and household use in this dry, hot country.

Although there are some isolated homesteads, most rural communities are nucleated settlements rather than dispersed farmsteads; that is, the farmer leaves his village to cultivate the fields outside it. The pattern holds for farming communities in the Kurdish highlands of the northeast as well as for those in the alluvial plain. The size of the settlement varies, generally with the volume of water available for household use and with the amount of land accessible to village dwellers. Sometimes, particularly in the lower Tigris and Euphrates valleys, soil salinity restricts the area of arable land and limits the size of the community dependent on it, and it also usually results in large unsettled and uncultivated stretches between villages.

Fragmentary information suggests that most farmers in the alluvial plain tend to live in villages of over 100 persons. For example, in the mid-1970s a substantial number of the residents of Baqubah, the administrative center and major city of Diyala Governorate, were employed in agriculture.

The Marsh Arabs (the Madan) of the south usually live in small clusters of two or three houses kept above water by rushes that are constantly being replenished. Such clusters often are close together, but access from one to another is possible only by small boats. Here and there a few natural islands permit slightly larger clusters. Some of these people are primarily water buffalo herders and lead a semi-nomadic life. In the winter, when the waters are at a low point, they build fairly large temporary villages. In the summer they move their herds out of the marshes to the river banks. Before the Marshes were drained, the lifestyle of the Madan centered around agriculture, particularly cultivating rice and dates, weaving read mats, raising water buffalo, and fishing. A form of local commerce had developed involving mostly local trade, supported by the use of small boats for transportation.
During the last two decades, and especially in the 1990s, the Madan have either migrated to settled communities away from the marshes or have been forced by government decree to relocate within the marshes.

Similarly, settlement patterns in the northern Kurdish areas have been affected during the last two decades; as a result, rural Kurds flocked into the regional centers of Arbil and Sulaymaniyah. The majority of Kurdish villages, however, remained intact.

In the arid parts of Iraq to the west and south, cities and large towns are almost invariably situated on watercourses, usually on the major rivers or their larger tributaries. In the south, this dependence has had its disadvantages. Until the recent development of flood control, Baghdad and other cities were subject to the threat of inundation. Moreover, the dikes needed for protection have effectively prevented the expansion of the urban areas in some directions. The growth of Baghdad, for example, was restricted by dikes on its eastern edge. The diversion of water to the Tharthar depression and the construction of a canal transferring water from the Tigris north of Baghdad to the Diyala River have permitted the irrigation of land outside the limits of the dikes and the expansion of settlements.

3. Land and Water Resources

3.1. Land Resources

It is estimated that 11.48 million hectares, or 26% of the total area of the country, are cultivable. The total area estimated to be used for agriculture is 8 million ha, which is almost 93% of the cultivable area. However, due to soil salinity, fallow practices and the unstable political situation it is estimated that only 3 to 5 million ha are actually cultivated annually. In 1993, the area actually cultivated was estimated at about 3.73 million ha, of which 3.46 million ha consisted of annual crops and 0.27 million ha consisted of permanent crops.

Cultivable area ~ 11.48 m ha.

Land area actually cultivated ~ 3-5 m ha.

Irrigated area ~ 1.9 m ha.

3.2. Land Use

Historically the most significant types of land use and food production in Iraq have been irrigated agriculture, which requires substantial investment and is an intensive form of land use; and pastoralism, which requires relatively little investment and is extensive. These have been combined with dryland farming in the semi-arid areas of northern Iraq. Although these basic types are technologically very different, they have been closely interrelated, socially and economically, for thousands of years.

Historical evidence shows some significant declines in production from time to time during the last five thousand years, but the causes (which appear in most cases to have involved a combination of both human and natural factors) have not been reconstructed convincingly. The old Mesopotamian systems, as well as the new one in present-day Iraq, have gone through several cycles of growth and decline.

Environmental problems in development generally derive not from basic technologies such as types of irrigation or grazing, but from the scale of the productive activity in relation to the resource. Before the first attempt to develop irrigation in modern-day Iraq, irrigation (which probably developed in its most primitive form not long after the domestication of plants and animals, some ten thousand years ago elsewhere in Mesopotamia) had already served as the basis of vast agricultural projects, and had had environmental effects which reduced productivity seriously. The best known example is from Mesopotamia; it was generally restricted to flood plains and was seasonal, depending on the annual flooding of the Tigris and Euphrates.

Perennial irrigation in Iraq, which requires storage and gradual release of the water through the period of minimum flow, is largely the introduction of the 20th century. Such irrigation has allowed major increases in areas under cultivation and intensification of cropping but it also magnifies the adverse effects of irrigation: soil salinity and waterlogging develop faster and some of the adverse effects are more difficult to reverse.

3.3. Land Degradation

More than 50% of Iraq's land area is desert, and an increasing part of the permanent pasture areas is subject to erosion because of reduced vegetation cover. Additionally, much of the cropland is losing its inherent productivity due to poor agricultural practices and over exploitation. The direct loss of agricultural land is most acute around urban centers, where established agricultural land is being lost to alternative uses, including urbanization, industrialization, and transport infrastructure. To compensate for this, new land is being brought into production through reclamation. The productivity of the reclaimed land, however, is in many cases only a fraction of the old, and new land is being brought into production more slowly than old land is being lost.

Overgrazing in desert areas is a major cause of plant cover loss, particularly in the semi-desert, which suffered a particularly severe loss of vegetation as a result of overgrazing, off-road vehicles, construction, and tourist activities.

3.4. River Basins

There is only one river basin in Iraq, the Shatt Al-Arab basin. The Shatt Al-Arab is the river formed by the confluence downstream of the Euphrates and the Tigris which flows into the Persian Gulf after a course of only 190 km. Before their confluence, the Euphrates flows for about 1,000 km and the Tigris for about 1,300 km, respectively, within the Iraqi territory. Nevertheless, due to the importance of the Euphrates and the Tigris, the country is generally divided into three river basins: the Tigris, the Euphrates, and the Shatt Al-Arab.

3.5. Surface Water Resources

Water resources in Iraq are controlled by the twin rivers, the Tigris and the Euphrates. Both are international rivers originating their source in Turkey. The Tigris river basin in Iraq has a total area of 253,000 km², or 54% of the total river basin area.

The average annual flow of the Euphrates as it enters Iraq is estimated at 30 km³, with a fluctuating annual value ranging from 10 to 40 km³. Unlike the Tigris, the Euphrates receives no tributaries within Iraq's borders.

For the Tigris, average annual runoff as it enters Iraq is estimated at 21.2 km³. All upstream and downstream tributaries of the Tigris are on its left bank; these are:

- The Greater Zab, which originates in Turkey and is partly regulated by the Bakhma dam. It generates 13.18 km³ at its confluence with the Tigris; 62% of the 25,810 km² of river basin is in Iraq;
- The Lesser Zab, which originates in Iran and is equipped with the Dokan dam (6.8 km³). The river basin of 21,475 km² (of which 74% is in Iraqi territory) generates about 7.17 km³ of water;
- Al-Adhaim (Great River), which drains about 13,000 km² entirely in Iraq. It generates about 0.79 km³ at its confluence with the Tigris. It is an intermittent stream subject to flash floods;
- Diyala, which originates in Iran and drains about 31,896 km², 75% of which is in Iraqi territory. It is equipped with the Darbandikhan dam and generates about 5.74 km³ at its confluence with the Tigris;
- Nahr Al-Tib, Dewarege and Shehabi rivers, with a combined draining of more than 8,000 km². They originate in Iran and bring together in the Tigris about 1 km³ of highly saline waters;
- Al-Karkha, whose course is mainly in Iran and, from a drainage area of 46,000 km², brings about 6.3 km³ yearly into Iraq, namely into the Hawr Al Hawiza during the flood season, and into the Tigris river during the dry season.

The Karun river, originating in Iran flows with its mean annual flow of 24.7 km³ into the Shatt Al-Arab. It brings a large amount of fresh water into the Shatt Al-Arab just before it reaches the Persian Gulf.

The Euphrates and the Tigris are subject to large and possibly disastrous floods. The level of water in the Tigris can rise at the rate of over 30 cm/hour. In the southern part of the country, immense areas are regularly inundated, levees often collapse, and villages and roads must be built on high embankments. The Tharthar reservoir was planned *inter alia* in the 1950s to protect Baghdad from the ravages of the periodic flooding of the Tigris.

3.6. Groundwater resources

Good quality subterranean water has been found in the foothills of the mountains in the northeast of the country and in the area along the right bank of the Euphrates:

- The aquifer in the northeast of the country has an estimated sustainable discharge of between 10 and 40 m^3/s, at depths of five to fifty meters. Its salinity increases towards the south-east of the area, where it reaches 1 mg/1;
- The aquifers on the right bank of the Euphrates river are found at depths up to 300 m, and have an estimated discharge of 13 m^3/s. Salinity varies between 4-6 dS/m.

In other areas of the country, groundwater is also found, but always with a salinity level higher than 10 dS/m.

3.7. Dams

In 1977, the on-river dams, all of which are located in the Tigris river basin, had a total capacity of 13.7 km^3. An important program of dam construction occurred in Iraq in the 1980s. The program consisted of the construction of an additional dam on the Tigris (11.1 km^3), the Qadisiah multipurpose dam on the Euphrates (8.2 km^3), the Bakhma dam on the upper Zab [one of the Tigris tributaries (17.1 km^3)], the Badush dam on the Tigris (0.5 km), and several other desert dams totaling about 0.5 km^3. The total on-river storage capacities for the Tigris will thus amount to 42 km^3, and 8.2 km^3 for the Euphrates. However, the Bakhma dam was completely destroyed. At present, the Al-Adom dam on the Tigris, with a capacity of 3.8 km^3, is under construction.

Two off-river storage lakes were created with the construction of the Tharthar dam (85 km^3) in the Tigris river basin, filled with the Wadi Tharthar waters and, since 1985, with Euphrates waters, and the Habbaniya dam (3.3 km^3), which can be filled from upstream Euphrates waters and which drains into the Euphrates downstream.

3.8. New watercourses

In order to increase water transport efficiency, minimize losses and waterlogging, and improve water quality, a number of new watercourses were constructed, especially in the southern part of the country. The Third river functions as a main out-fall drain collecting drainage waters of more than 1.5 million hectares of agricultural land north of Baghdad to the Persian Gulf. Completed in December 1992, the length of the watercourse is 565 km, with a total discharge of 210 m³/s. Other watercourses were also constructed to reclaim new lands or to reduce waterlogging.

3.9. Water withdrawal

Total water withdrawal is estimated at 42.8 km³ in 1990, of which 92% is for agricultural purposes, 3% for domestic use and the remaining 2% for industrial use. According to the most recent estimates (1999), 85 % of river water withdrawal is used for agricultural purposes.

3.10. Irrigation and drainage

The history of irrigation started 7500 years ago in the land between the Tigris and the Euphrates when the Sumerians built a canal to irrigate wheat and barley. Irrigation potential was estimated in 1990 at over 5.5 million ha, of which 63% in the Tigris basin, 35% in the Euphrates basin, and 2% in the Shatt Al-Arab basin. Considering the soil resources, it is estimated that about 6 million hectares are classified as excellent, good or moderately suitable for flood irrigation. With the development of water storage facilities, the regulated flow has increased and changed the irrigation potential significantly, since it was estimated at 4.25 million hectares only in 1976. However, irrigation development depends to a large extent on the volume of water released by the upstream countries.

3.11. Irrigated areas

The total water managed area was estimated at 3.5 million ha in 1990, all of it being equipped for full or partial control irrigation.

The areas irrigated by surface water are estimated at 3.305m ha, of which 105,000 ha (3 %) are in the Shatt Al-Arab river basin, 2.2m ha (67%) in the Tigris river basin, and 1m ha (30%) in the Euphrates river basin. However, it should be noted that all these areas are not actually irrigated, since a large part has been abandoned due to waterlogging and salinity. Only 1,936,000 ha were estimated to be actually irrigated in 1993. The areas irrigated from groundwater were estimated at 220,000 ha in 1990, with some 18,000 wells. About 8,000 ha were reported equipped for micro-irrigation, but these techniques were not used.

3.12. Salinity

Salinity has always been a major issue in both old Mesopotamia and modern-day Iraq and it was already recorded as a cause of crop yield reductions some 3,800 years ago. By 1,700 BC, salt levels in soils throughout southern Mesopotamia were so high that no wheat was grown. In Iraq, the shift from wheat to barley was accompanied by a serious decline in fertility (attributed to salinization). In Girsu, yields were 253.7 m^3/km^2 in 2400 BC; 146. m^3/km^2 by 2100 BC, and 89.7 m^3/km^2 in 1700 BC. In southern Iraq, about 3500 BC, wheat and barley were nearly equal in area. In 2500 BC, however, the less-salt-tolerant wheat accounted for 1/6 of the cropped area, and by 2100 BC it accounted for 2% of the cropped area in the Girsu region. By 1700 BC, wheat had been abandoned completely in the southern part of the alluvium plains.

Three major occurrences of salinity have been established from ancient records. The earliest and most serious affected southern Iraq from 2400 BC to 1700 BC.; a milder salinity problem occurred in central Iraq from 1300-900 BC.; and finally, the Nahrawan area east of Baghdad became salty only after 1200 AD. With the converging effects of mounting maintenance requirements and the declining capacity for more than rudimentary maintenance tasks, the virtual desertion of the lower Diyala area of Mesopotamia was inevitable. By the middle of the 12th century AD, most of the Nahrawan region was already abandoned. Mongol horsemen arrived a century later, but are blamed for the devastation they found ever since.

Mesopotamians, some 5-7 thousand year ago, selected arable land for wheat and barley cultivation close to the rivers and dug ditches to the Tigris and Euphrates to irrigate them. Despite a two-year cropping cycle which left the land fallow for two summers after each winter cultivation, productivity was quickly impaired by increasing salinity, and the people moved regularly to new areas. By 1950, approximately 60 per cent of Iraq's agricultural land was estimated to be seriously affected by salinity; and 20-30 per cent had been abandoned with the rate of loss estimated at 1 per cent per year.

Salinity problems were recorded in Mesopotamia some 3,800 years ago.

Almost 75% of Iraq's irrigated land suffers from salinity problems.

Throughout the seven thousand year history of this system under various populations, salinity had been a recurrent problem, which the traditional technology could not counteract except by long-term fallowing or abandonment. However, this historical record appears not to have influenced the perceptions of modern development planners.

It was estimated that in 1970 half the irrigated areas in central and southern Iraq were degraded due to waterlogging and salinity. The absence of drainage facilities and, to a lesser extent, the irrigation practices used (i.e., flooding) were the major causes of these problems. In 1978, a land rehabilitation program was undertaken, comprising concrete lining for irrigation canals, installation of field drains and collector drains. By 1989, a total of 750,000 ha had been reclaimed at a cost of around $US 2,000/ha.

Recent estimations have nevertheless shown that 4% of the irrigated areas were severely saline, 50% medium saline and 20% slightly saline; i.e. a total of 74% of the irrigated areas suffered from some degree of salinity. The Ministry of Irrigation estimated at 17 million tons the amount of salt transported to the Persian Gulf by the New River in 1995. Irrigation with highly saline waters (~ 12 dS/m) has been practiced for date palm trees since 1977. The use of brackish groundwater is also reported for tomato irrigation in the south of the country.

Recently, however, (1999) vast expanses of waterlogged lands and white sheets of salt stretching across fields of the main irrigated regions of Iraq have been reported. In one estimate, about half of the 750,000 ha reclaimed earlier have turned back to marshy lands unsuitable for agriculture. The other half also faces similar prospects unless proper measures are taken to drain excess water.

Approximately 20-30% of Iraq's potentially irrigable land is unusable, i.e. has been converted to desert by salination of irrigation projects. Viewed from the air, vast areas of southern Iraq glisten with salt like new-fallen snow

Southern Iraq has been ruined by millennia of poorly engineered irrigation systems. The ground water in middle Iraq is already at 15 dS/m, approximately 80% of the irrigated land around Baghdad is affected by salinity, and in the south it is almost as salty as sea water, at 35 dS/m.

3.13. Trends in Water Resources Management

During the last forty years there has been a dramatic change in the way water from the Tigris and Euphrates was utilized in agriculture. Dams were built on both rivers and storage capacities increased to the point that total water storage capacity in Turkey alone exceeds the annual flow of both rivers within its boundaries. Similarly, and since the 1960s, there has been a change from excess water availability to a situation in which there may not be enough water to meet the planned requirements of Turkey, Syria, and particularly, Iraq.

Geographic factors contributed to Iraq's water problems. Like all rivers, the Tigris and the Euphrates carry large amounts of silt downstream. This silt is deposited in river channels, in canals, and on flood plains. In Iraq, the soil is moderate to high in salinity. As the water table rises through flooding or irrigation, salt rises into the topsoil, rendering agricultural land unproductive. In addition, the alluvial silt is highly saline. Drainage thus becomes very necessary. However, Iraq's terrain is very flat. Baghdad for example, although 550 km from the Persian Gulf, is only 34 meters above sea level. This slight gradient makes the plains susceptible to flooding and, although facilitates irrigation, it also hampers drainage. The flat terrain also provides relatively few sites for dams. Most importantly, Iraq lies downstream from both Syria and Turkey on the Euphrates, and downstream from Turkey on the Tigris. Iraq claimed that the irrigated area along the Euphrates dropped by 126,000 ha as a result of water works during 1974-1975 in Turkey and Syria.

Iraq's water problems are caused by geographic, topographic, and management factors.

Major structural adjustments are needed to solve Iraq's water problems.

Two major dams were built during the 1980s to irrigate agricultural lands in the Jezira area in the north and the central parts of the flood plains in Iraq. The Mosul dam was built on the Tigris in late 1980 to irrigate the Jezira area with a capacity of 10.7 billion cubic meters. The Hadeetha dam, built on the Euphrates were started in 1978 and completed in 1985, with a capacity of 6.4 billion cubic meters. Additional major flood control and irrigation projects in Iraq include 10 dams and 5 regulators, with a combined discharge capacity of 64,000 m3 per second. Additionally, Wadi Tharthar and Habbaniah lake are used to store irrigation water with a combined storage capacity of 853.25 million cubic meters.

Two main irrigation projects were planned in 1990: the first irrigation project in central Iraq, supplied by waters from the Third River, was designed for a total area of 250,000 ha, and the Jezira irrigation project was planned to cover an area of 325,000 ha. The Um Almaarik river in the southwest region was expected to irrigate 20,000 ha upon completion. However, the development of irrigation as it was planned in the upstream countries, particularly the southeast Anatolian (GAP) project in Turkey, and the irrigation projects in Syria, substantially reduced Iraqi irrigation potential. Since water shortages are forecast to occur with the development of irrigation, solutions have to be found for an integrated basin-level planning of water resources development.

Although Iraq has known for almost 20 years that it would face smaller water amounts once the Turkish and Syrian irrigation schemes were completed, there is little evidence to suggest that Iraq has planned any formal adjustments to its own irrigated areas, especially on the Euphrates. Its response seems to have been to leave it to the local governorates to cope as best they can with the smaller water volumes. This seems to imply that the more difficult areas to irrigate in any region will be abandoned first, thereby causing the total irrigated crop area to contract.

Solutions to immediate and future water management problems, in the Tigris-Euphrates basin within Iraq, may call for major structural adjustment in the agricultural sector. In the short-term, it seems inevitable that there will be land abandonment along the Euphrates as Turkey's use of the Euphrates increases. Iraq has to come to terms quickly with a changing situation in which available water amounts along the Euphrates will steadily decline. However, this will have economic and social impacts on the rural population of Iraq. In the lower part of the basin, rural areas will not be able to sustain the same high level of population that has been the case in the past. This might suggest that rural de-population will increase, putting further pressures on the already crowded urban centers.

Another main issue in water resources management is protection of water quality. The level of salinity in the Euphrates river is high and is expected to increase with the development of irrigation in

33

the basin and, as a consequence, the diminution of the water flow, particularly in the dry season.

Treatment of municipal and industrial wastewater is considered as one way to preserve river water quality. Reuse of treated wastewater for irrigation was also envisaged before 1990. Some industries are already obliged to desalinate the Euphrates waters before using them.

Other measures which could be undertaken would need regional cooperation for better management of the flood waters and the dams. But the regulation capacities on the Euphrates are already greater than the entire average flow because of the lack of coordination between the riparian countries (Turkey, Syria and Iraq).

4. Soils of Iraq

Geologically, most of Iraq is underlain by rocks of the Cretaceous and Eocene eras, mainly limestone, with bands of salt and gypsum. On the lowland plains of the twin rivers, the surface is covered by fluvial deposits and alluvium. In these latter areas azonal, alluvial, hydromorphic, irrigated soils are found. In the west and south, zonal desert-steppe soils are found, sometimes stony, sometimes sandy and often calcareous. The mountain soils of the north are varied – red, brown, and chestnut forest soils – and in places are merely skeletal where rock outcrops occur. Gypsum is often present in the red and brown soils of the plains and foothills.

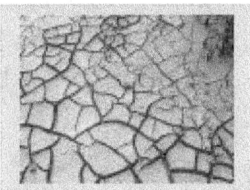

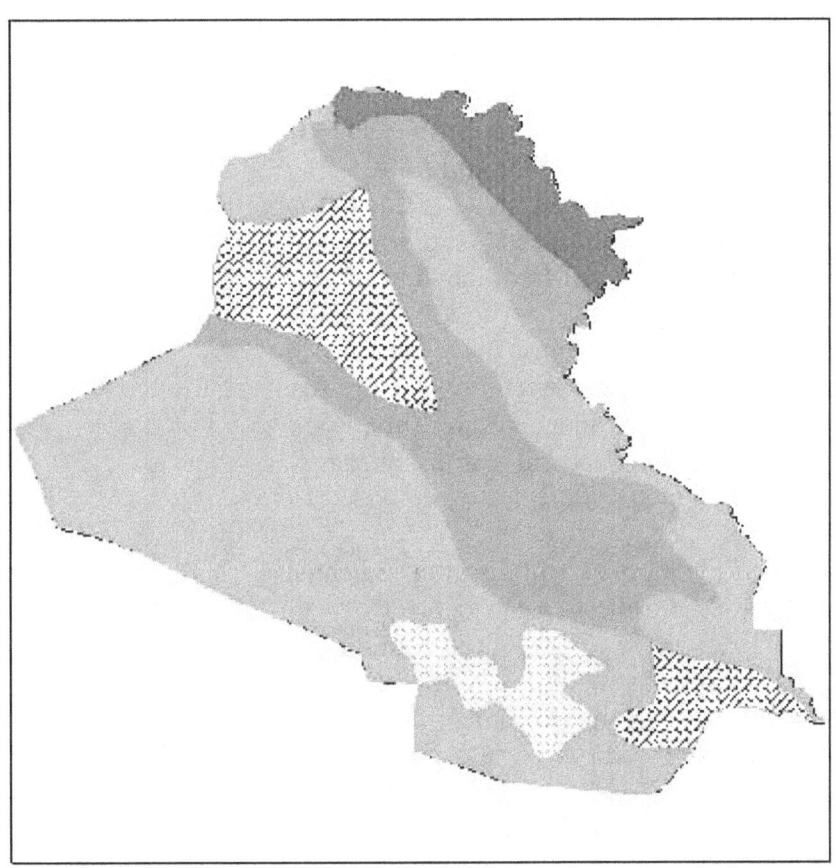

Fig. Major soils in Iraq.

The area of gypsiferous soils in Iraq was estimated at 12,503,000 ha or 28.6% of agricultural soils in the country (or 6.7% of all gypsiferous soils in the world). These soils are mainly associated with a geological substratum containing gypsum and anhydrite inter-layers or with Pleistocene terraces connected with such deposits. The basin of Iraq was partly filled with detrital sediments during the Lower Miocene. Inland seas were formed at this time in

Gypsiferous soils predominate (28.6%) in the Euphrates basin.

which, on evaporation, gypsum, and limestone were formed characterizing the Lower Fars Series of the Middle Miocene; this geological formation is the origin of most gypsiferous soils in Iraq.

Gypsiferous soils are well represented in the Euphrates river basin in Iraq, where three groups of gypsiferous soils can be distinguished; these are: soils with less than 10 percent gypsum (slightly gypsiferous) suitable for all crops; soils with 10-15 percent gypsum (moderately gypsiferous) suitable for limited number of crops, and soil with 25-50 percent gypsum (highly gypsiferous) not suitable for irrigated agriculture.

Data on gypsiferous soils in Iraq indicated that a 3 to 10 percent of gypsum content does not interfere significantly with soil characteristics such as structure, consistency and water holding capacity; while in soils containing 10 to 25 percent of gypsum, the gypsum crystals tend to break the continuity of the soil mass.

The percentage of clay in gypsiferous soils depends on the kind of soil developed. In the Typic Gypsiorthids of Iraq, the clay content rarely exceeds 20 percent by weight and the cation exchange capacity ranges between 7 and 14 meq/100 g of soil. However, in Calcic Gypsiorthids with a calcic horizon overlying the gypsic layer and smaller amounts of gypsum, the clay content ranges between 20 and 50 percent by weight, and cation exchange capacity ranges between 14 and 18 meq/100 g.

Intensive field observations of gypsiferous soils in Iraq indicated that root growth was inhibited where the gypsum content of soil was over 10 percent. This is apparently because of the poor air and water infiltration caused by poor soil structure. It was also found that soils containing more than 25 percent gypsum in the rooting zone result in poor plant growth. In the spring, wheat crops wilt on shallow gypsiferous soils when other crops on deeper soils show no signs of distress. Roots do not penetrate the gypsum layer, even when it is quite wet.

5. The Agrarian Structures

5.1. Institutional Environment

The Ministry of Agriculture is responsible for organizing the ownership of agricultural lands, contracts with farmers, cooperatives and agricultural companies in addition to enhancing agricultural investment activities. In particular, the Ministry is responsible for providing agricultural inputs to all farmers, and for marketing the agricultural commodities.

The Ministry of Irrigation is in charge of water resources development, irrigation and drainage development, as well as their operation and maintenance. Its major functions are to assess water requirements and resources; control running water, reservoirs, wetlands and marshes, underground water; the construction of dams, canals and drainage systems; soil conservation, classification; land evaluation and use; and research and studies on land and water. The Ministry is executing most of the water resources development projects with the assistance of a number of State-owned companies.

5.2. Land Reform

Iraq is one of the least densely populated countries in the Middle East, but has the greatest agricultural potential. Unfortunately, the physical developments of irrigation schemes, crop innovations or introductions of the "green revolution" have failed to produce a brave new world for agriculture in Iraq and other countries in the Middle East. During most of the 20th century, the skewed nature of land ownership was well documented in Iraq; and the combination of uneven distribution of land and a farm management structure that frequently divorced owners from day-to-day operations kept cultivation techniques at an apparently primitive level.

During the last 40 years, the agrarian sector witnessed major drastic measures.

- land reform
- Cooperative farms
- Collective State Farms
- Central Planning
- Private ownership

Share-cropping practices varied greatly depending on the cultural regime, whether dryland or irrigated farming was in question, and depending on how many factors of production – land, water, seed, draft animals and labor -- the land owners provided. The share-cropper may end up taking as little as 20% of the crop he cultivated.

The key to solving problems of Iraqi agriculture, after the revolution in 1958, was felt to lie in the introduction of land reform by which the cultivated area could be redistributed or consolidated and the sector opened up for modernization. Moreover, political objectives were considered, including destruction of the power of landlord classes and the imposition of central control on the rural population.

Land reform (referred to as Agrarian Reform in Iraq, Syria and Egypt) came as a part of the reform measures introduced by the successive post-independence, "revolutionary" governments of Iraq.

Performance of the land reform agency in Iraq, where motivations were above all political and the bureaucracy altogether inadequate to handle the enormous burden of administration, was far from satisfactory. The pre-reform agrarian system was deficient in many ways, but subsequent research showed that land reform was no cure, and reform activities probably diminished security of tenure, reduced peasant initiative, undermined private farming enterprise, and inhibited growth in output from the cultivated area in Iraq.

The two main features of implementation of agrarian reform were inability of the successive Iraqi governments to redistribute lands so readily expropriated from former owners and yet a commitment to creeping bureaucratization of the countryside. On the one hand, farmers were deprived of freedom of action or reasonable access to necessary inputs, such as fertilizer and seed, or participation in marketing, while on the other hand, they were not provided with effective new management structures and supporting services by the government. In 1979, approximately 0.4m farmers were organized in 1,987 cooperatives. As a consequence, rural depopulation rates were high, and erratic and falling farm outputs were observed in the wake of continuing land reforms.

In addition to land reform, large tracts of land were handed to the "socialist sector" in agriculture. In 1981, the relative share of this sector in Iraqi agriculture was 39%.

However, in 1981, the Iraqi government appeared to change its policy and reduced direct government involvement in farming. Farmers no longer had to belong to local cooperatives in order to have access to credit, supplies and equipment. Some cooperatives and a few state farms still exist, however, with the state farms being used to demonstrate new technologies, produce certified seed and handle industrial crops (e.g., cotton) that require a large area of land for efficient production.

In conclusion, Iraq's system of land tenure and inefficient government implementation of land reform contributed to the low productivity and the slow growth of the agricultural sector. By 1987, the government expressed disappointment at the slow pace of agricultural development, conceding that collectivized state farms were not profitable and announced plans to privatize agriculture by leasing or selling state farms to the private sector.

6. Biodiversity and Plant Genetic Resources

6.1. Biodiversity

Four vegetational zones are recognized in Iraq: the desert, the steppe, the mountain forest and the Alpine regions. However, desert and steppe regions are not readily discernible. Low rainfall plays a dominant role in the formation of the short-lived herbaceous plants in the last two zones. Arboreal types are practically absent in the steppe and deserts of Iraq.

The northern part of the country, with its mountains and available rainfall, sustains virgin forests, man-made forests, and a large number of crop plants and their wild relatives. Over cutting and overgrazing in the Zagros Mountains have reduced some of Iraq's oak forests to scrublands. Stands of other trees – maple, hawthorn, and pistachio, for example – remain, however. Alpine plants that can survive harsh weather appear at higher elevations.

Indigenous plant and animal life in Iraq is under increasing threat due to the impact of development. Overgrazing and mismanagement of rangelands have led to the loss of natural plant cover. Deforestation is now a major concern in the northern highlands and mountains.

> *Iraq harbors four vegetational zones:*
>
> *-The Desert*
> *-The Steppe*
> *-The Mountains*
> *-The Alpine Regions*

Reeds, boxthorns, buttercups, rushes, and saltbush grow in the plains and marshes. Date palms thrive in many parts of the country, and occasionally poplars and willows are found in the plains.

Centuries of human settlement have depleted Iraq's wildlife. Wildlife, such as fallow deer, ostrich, wild goat, and antelope, have been extinct by the turn of the 20th century due to indiscriminate hunting. The threat to wildlife was worsened through the destruction of their habitats, particularly deforestation. The country lost at least 10 per cent of its remaining natural forest during the 1980s.

> *In Iraq, there are 81 mammalian species, one endemic, and 381 bird species, one endemic.*

On the whole, there is little information on wild animal species, and reliable data are generally limited to certain mammals and birds In the 1990s, UNDP estimated that only one of each of the 81 known mammalian and the 381 known bird species in Iraq are endemic.

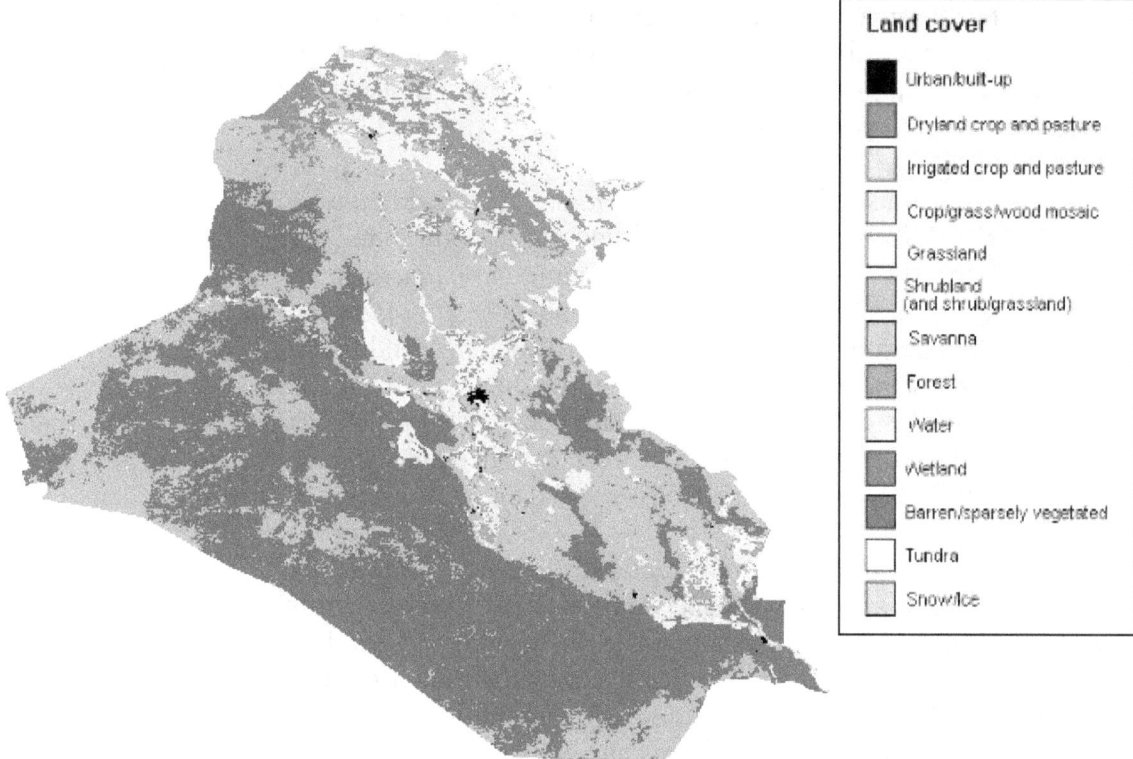

Fig. 8. Land cover in Iraq.

Surviving mammals include bats, rats, jackals, hyenas and wildcats. Among Iraq's domesticated animals are camels, oxen, water buffalo and horses. Northern Iraqis raise large flocks of sheep and goats for their milk, meat, wool and skin.

6.2. Plant Genetic Resources:

Plant genetic resources activities in Iraq began in 1977 through a collaborative initiative between the Iraqi Ministry of Agriculture, IBPGR and FAO. A modest genebank facility was built at Abu Ghraib, Baghdad, with the assistance of both international organizations.

Field work, and conservation and evaluation activities did not start, however, until the mid-1980s. Approximately 1,400 accessions of local material are stored under medium-term storage conditions. Wheat and barley make up 40% of the collection, with the remaining portion composed of food legumes, forage legumes, vegetable crops and oil crops.

Wild relatives of wheat and barley can be found in northern Iraq.

The grasses are an interesting genetic resource in Iraq. In this dry and arid part of the Old World, these plants have a special condensed form of life compared with plants inhabiting milder

41

climates. In Mesopotamia, the sever cold, especially in the north, is followed by a very short spring season, which in turn leads to an extremely long, hot summer. Consequently, grasses complete their life cycle within a period of 3-4 months.

Most wild wheats (*Triticum dicoccoides, T. araraticum, T boeoticum*, and *T urartu*) can still be found in the north. Similarly, a large number of *Aegilops* species, including *Ae triuncialis, Ae crassa, Ae umbellulata, Ae biuncialis*, and *Ae spiltoides*, are widespread in most northern and central parts of Iraq. Wild barley (*Hordeum spontanaeum*) is abundant throughout most of the country. Landraces of wheat and barley still occupy a few niches in the dryland farming sector, although their replacement by pure-line, high-yielding varieties is on the rise.

The northern part of Iraq is a rich center of diversity for a number of stone fruit trees, both wild and domesticated. Evergreen fruit trees, including date palm, predominate in central and southern Iraq. A country-wide program was launched by the State Board for Agricultural Research and Faculties of Agriculture to collect, characterize, and evaluate genetic resources of a number of fruit species. These included pomegranate, pistachio, grape, olive, and apple. Field genebanks were established on a small scale in representative locations throughout the country.

The date palm enjoys a favorable status in Iraq. In the early 1980s, an estimated 30 million date palm trees were growing in Iraq, but the number has declined dramatically since then. Major efforts have been initiated for the proper conservation and propagation of the more than 700 varieties of date palm in Iraq. Traditional (offshoots) and modern propagation methods, including tissue culture, have been utilized to maintain and, finally, to enhance the genetic diversity and promote the cultivation of this ancient tree.

Iraq harbors a tremendous wealth of vegetables adapted to the various bioclimatic regions of the country. They include landraces of tomato, eggplant, okra, watermelon, melon, onion, cucumber, garlic, lettuce, cabbage and carrots. A nationwide project was initiated in 1986 to survey, collect and evaluate genetic resources of Iraqi vegetables, enhance their yield potential through pure line selection; and distribute improved lines to farmers. Landraces of vegetable crops were collected and conserved; the genetic diversity of most crops, especially the cross-pollinated ones, was improved; and high-yielding, more adapted, pure lines of vegetables derived from local landraces were distributed to farmers.

The predominant species in the north forests of Iraq is *Quercus,* with *Q. aegilopoides, Q. aegilopoides infectoria* and *Q. aegilopoides-libani* representing the species. There are three forest formations in this part of the country. In a few isolated areas of Iraq, such as Jabal Sinjar, a forth forest formation dominated by *Pinus halepensis* var *brutia* can be found. Other forest species growing throughout the mountains of Iraq are *Juniperus oxycedrus, Pistacia mutica* and *Prunus orientalis*. Many scientists are concerned that the genetic resources of Iraq's forest trees have not been adequately surveyed and collected. They suggest that there is an urgent need for a preliminary survey and assessment.

The need for cold storage facilities (short-, medium-, and long-term cold rooms) is urgent. Also, there is a need for seed processing and testing equipment. In addition, training of manpower is essential for the long-term viability of plant genetic resources work in the country.

7. Crops

Agricultural production, which, at one time, employed about a third of the workforce, is not sufficient to meet the country's food requirements. Iraq's chief crops include wheat, barley, rice, vegetables, dates (Iraq is one of the world's largest producers), and cotton. Crop production accounted for about two-thirds of value added in the agricultural sector in the late 1980s.

Planting of the winter crops, which normally starts in the second half of October, is occasionally delayed due to inadequate rainfall early in the season. Production is also likely to be constrained by the serious shortages of essential agricultural inputs. Last year (2001), in addition to the shortage of agricultural inputs, a severe drought and the widespread incidence of pests and weeds adversely affected cereal crops. Total cereal output in 1999 was estimated at 1.6 million tons, nearly 40 percent below the previous five-year average.

Iraq produces 30% of its total needs of cereals.

Drought, lack of inputs and pests reduce crop yields by 50-70%.

A severe drought coupled with serious shortages of essential agricultural inputs and the widespread pest and weed infestations have adversely affected the 1999 winter crops. Nearly 1.2 million hectares under cereals, about 46 % of the total cultivated area, have been severely damaged.

Two consecutive years of severe drought and inadequate availability of essential agricultural inputs have adversely affected the Iraqi agriculture. Reflecting a substantial reduction in plantings and yields, cereal production in 2000 was substantially below the 1999 poor harvest. In the most affected areas (central and southern Iraq), not only were the plantings reduced, but also some 75 percent of the cropped area under wheat and barley was heavily damaged and were mostly grazed by livestock. Cereal yields in 2000 were reduced to all time low levels. In northern Governorates, insufficient and erratic rainfall continued during much of the 1999/2000 crop season, with only one-third of the normal rainfall received in parts of northern Iraq.

Despite crop intensification, cropping density is less than 50%.

Drought conditions also drastically reduced the water resources in rivers, dams, lakes and canals, some of which have virtually dried up. As a result, prospects are unfavorable for the upcoming irrigated summer crops.

Despite improved precipitation in the region, prospects for the 2002 winter grain crops in Iraq are uncertain. Cereal production will be affected by serious shortages of fertilizers, spare parts for agricultural machinery and other agricultural inputs. Production of cereals (mainly wheat and barley) in 2001 is estimated at 1.8 million tons, 12 percent below average.

Most farming in Iraq entails planting and harvesting a single crop per year. In the rainfed areas the winter crops, primarily small grains, are planted in the fall and harvested in late spring or early summer. In the irrigated areas of central and southern Iraq, summer crops predominate.

Even with some double or triple cropping, the intensity of cultivation is usually on the order of 50 percent because of the practice of leaving about half the arable land fallow each year. In the rainfed region, land is left fallow so that it can accumulate moisture. The fertility of fallow land is also increased by plowing under weeds and other plant material that grow during the fallow period. On irrigated land, fallow periods also contribute some humus to the soil.

7.1. Small Grains

Small grains, primarily wheat and barley, are Iraq's most important crops. Cereal production increased almost 80 percent between 1975 and 1985, notwithstanding the wide variations in the harvest from year to year as the amount and the timing of rainfall strongly affected both the area planted and crop yields. Between 1980 and 1985, the area under wheat increased steadily at a cumulative growth of 30 percent, to about 1,566,500 hectares. In 1985, Iraq harvested a bumper crop of 1.4 million tons of wheat. In 1984, a drought year, Iraq harvested less than half the planted area for a yield of between 250,000 and 471,000 tons, according to foreign and Iraqi sources, respectively. The north and central rain-fed parts of Iraq are the principal wheat producing regions. In 1991, there were 224,490 ha of irrigated wheat, with an average yield of 2.7 tons/ha, while the rainfed wheat area was estimated at 508,620 ha, with an average yield of 1.7 tons/ha.

Per capita consumption of cereals dropped from 191 in 1985 to 121 in 1998.

Up until 1990, domestic grain production accounted for only about 30% of total consumption, with the balance covered by imports. The estimated cost of food imports ranged from US$ 2-3 billion. Total consumption of cereals dropped from 6.694 million tons in 1984/1985 to 3.646 million tons in 1995/1996, then increased to 5.356 million tons in 1997/1998 after the implementation of the Oil-for-Food Program. Almost 50% of cereals (3.254 million tons) were imported during 1984/1985, resulting in a per capita cereal food use of 191 kg/year. In 1997/1998, however, the corresponding figures were 3.23 million tons and 179 kg/person/year. In 1995/1996, the sharp drop in domestic cereal production (2.42 million tons) and limitations on imported cereals (1.21 million tons), however, resulted in a very low per capita cereal food use (121 kg/year).

Fig. 9. Cereal production (metric tons) in Iraq during the period 1960-2000.

Production of wheat in the three Northern Governorates (Iraqi Kurdistan) is reported to have increased as a result of the increase in the use of fertilizer and pesticides which were distributed under the oil-for-food program. However, overall prospects for the cereal output remain uncertain in the Central and Southern Regions, mainly due to below average and unevenly distributed rains as well as shortages of essential agricultural inputs and the widespread incidence of pests, and weeds.

Barley requires less water than wheat does, and it is more tolerant of salinity in the soil. For these reasons, Iraq started to substitute barley production for wheat production in the 1970s, particularly in southern regions troubled by soil salinity. Between 1980 and 1985, the total area under barley grew by 44 percent, and by 1985, barley and wheat were virtually equal in terms of area cultivated and total yield. In 1991, there were 200,770 ha of irrigated barley, with an average yield of 1.8 tons/ha, while the rainfed barley area was estimated at 323,730 ha, with an average yield of 1.3 tons/ha.

Rice, grown in paddies, was Iraq's third most important crop as measured by cultivated area, which in 1985 amounted to 24,500 hectares. The area under cultivation, however, did not grow appreciably between 1980 and 1985; the 1985 production totaled almost 150,000 tons. Iraq also produced maize, millet, and oil seeds (e.g., sesame) in smaller quantities.

Fig. 10. Cereal yield in Iraq during the period 1960-2000.

7.2. Food Legumes

Lentils, chickpeas, and to some extent, broad beans, are an important part of the Iraqi diet. However, production of these legumes declined dramatically in the 1990s. Originally almost a self sufficient in lentils and chickpeas, Iraq now imports >40% of local requirements for lentils and >50% of local requirements for chickpeas. Farmers stopped producing lentils and chickpeas because of low yields and rising labor costs. Most lentil farmers use manual labor almost exclusively, and labor shortages during harvest result in crop losses. Dryland farmers are switching to other crops, mostly cereals, to increase profits, simply because cereal growing is almost fully mechanized and less expensive to grow. To increase the production of lentils and chickpeas, increase farmers' incomes, and reduce Iraq's protein food deficit, Iraqi

Food legumes lag behind cereals in area and production

47

researchers, in cooperation with ICARDA, developed improved varieties of food legumes as part of a package of effective technologies and agricultural practices.

7.3. Industrial Crops

A number of other crops are grown, but acreage and production were limited. With the exception of tobacco, of which Iraq produced 17,000 tons on 16,500 hectares in 1985, cash crop production declined steeply in the 1980s. Probably because of domestic competition from synthetic imports and a declining export market, production of cotton was only 7,200 tons in 1985, compared with 26,000 tons in 1977. Production of sugar beets was halted completely in 1983, and sugarcane production declined by more than half between 1980 and 1985. Iraq may have cut back on production of sugar beets and sugarcane because of an intention to produce sugar from dates.

7.4. Vegetables

Vegetable production also increased, particularly near urban centers, where a comparatively advanced marketing system had been developed. Vegetable gardening usually employed relatively modern techniques, including the use of chemical fertilizers and pesticides. Tomatoes were the most important crop, with production amounting to more than 600,000 tons in 1985. Other vegetables produced in significant quantity were beans, eggplant, okra, cucumbers, and onions. Overall vegetable production increased almost 90 percent between 1975 and 1985, even though the production of legumes dropped about 25 percent over the same period.

With food supplies available under the rationing system meeting only about one-third of the usual food energy needs of Iraqi people, vegetables and fruits have assumed increasing importance in the diet of the people. As a result, demand for and prices of vegetables have increased generating more attractive profit margins. Reflecting this development, there has been a renewed emphasis on vegetable production. The area devoted to vegetables has increased from about 8 per cent of the total cultivated area in 1989/90 to about 9 per cent in 1994/95. But the increase in area was largely offset by a decrease in yield and lower quality of the produce. Non-availability of vegetable seeds is by far the most important constraint, followed by a lack of plant protection chemicals and spray pumps, herbicides, and fertilizers mainly of compound types. Use of urea alone, when available, has been aggravating the alkalinity of the soils, resulting in low crop response and low yields. The main characteristics of vegetable fields include: low plant population because of poor seed quality and insufficient land preparation; weak plant growth because of low and unbalanced use of fertilizers; high percentage of damaged plants and fruits because of non-availability of plant protection chemicals and equipment; and low yield and poor quality because of the large scale weed infestation and insect attacks.

A tomato production improvement project aims to encourage farmers to plant green-house-grown tomato seedlings. These are of much higher quality than the traditionally grown tomato; they produce higher yields and this translates into increased income to farmers and greater supply of tomato in local markets.

Prior to the 1960's, less than a hundred hectares of potatoes were grown in Iraq. However, the area and production of potato increased dramatically, especially during the 1980s. Yield (t/ha) and area (ha) of potato are presented in the following Figure. Potatoes are grown mainly in the northern uplands around Mosul and the central valley of the Tigris and Euphrates rivers near Baghdad. Some potatoes are also grown in the lower Tigris-Euphrates Valley, but production there is limited by soil salinity.

There is no firm estimate of annual production of vegetables in Iraq. Estimates available through FAO Statistics indicate that it has varied between 3.2 and 3.5 million tons during 1991–1995.

7.5. Fruit Trees

The estimated number of fruit orchards including citrus, date palm, and a variety of other fruits in 1989 was 84,000 (with average numbers of trees per orchard of about 832 in 1989) compared to 219,000 in 1978. The estimated productive number of orchards in 1995 is about the same as in 1989, but the annual production has since increased, ranging from 1.1 to 1.2 million tons during 1990–1994. The total production in 1995 was about 1.3 million tons. Farmers put in extra efforts to manage their orchards during the 1990–1995 period, but to little or no avail. In the absence of necessary machinery and chemicals, farmers cannot do much against increasing weeds and infestation by insects and pests. In some areas also, orchards are suffering from waterlogging and salinity.

49

7.6. Date Palm

Dates, of which Iraq produces eight distinct varieties, have long been a staple in the local diet. The most abundant date groves are found along Shatt al Arab. More than 30 million date palms existed in the early 1960s. In the mid-1970s, the Iraqi government estimated that the number of date palms had declined to about 22 million, at which time production of dates amounted to 578,000 tons. The devastation of the Shatt al Arab area during the Iran-Iraq War hastened the destruction of date palm groves, and in 1985 the government estimated the number of date palms at fewer than 13 million. Date production in 1987 dropped to 220,000 tons. The government-managed Iraqi Date Administration, however, planned to increase production in an attempt to boost export revenue. In 1987 about 150,000 tons, or 68 percent of the harvest, was exported, primarily to Western Europe, Japan, India, and other Arab countries. The Iraqi Date Administration also devised plans to construct large facilities to extract sugar, alcohol, vinegar, and concentrated protein meal from dates. Iraq produced a variety of other fruits as well, including grapes, apples, apricots, and citrus. Production of such fruits increased almost 30 percent between 1975 and 1985.

Iraq is in the center of origin and center of diversity of date palm.

There are ~ 20 million date palm trees in Iraq, mainly in the south.

There are ~ 700 known date palm varieties in Iraq.

Salinity and insects are threatening date palms in Iraq.

Dates are the most important fruit in Iraq. Prior to 1990, about 400,000 tons of dates were exported annually. In addition, it is an important component in the food intake of the Iraqi people. Although export of dates is currently negligible, there is a strong domestic demand for them in view of their value as a supplementary food. Available statistics show that the number of date palm trees were damaged and reduced from 21.403 million in 1981 to 15.911 million in 1991. The estimated number of trees in 1995 is about 18 million. Under the current conditions of food shortage, there have been attempts by farmers to improve the management of date palm trees; they cannot, however, do very much as they lack machinery and spare parts, insecticides and herbicides.

Basra, in southern Iraq, is the major date palm growing area in the country; approximately 13 million date palm trees of over 400 varieties are grown here and cover an area of about 50,000 ha, the largest date palm "forest" in the world.

Date palm trees were, and still are, integral components of the farming systems in arid and semi-arid regions, especially in the oases of the Middle East whether in small farm units or as large scale plantations. The tremendous advantage of the "tree of life" is its resilience, its long term productivity, and its multiple purpose attributes. In Iraq, most date plantations are intercropped with vegetables, cereals or fodder crops in the first few years and subsequently with low growing fruit trees and grapevines. The fruits, depending upon the variety and growing conditions, vary in weight from 2 to 60 grams, in length from 2 to 11 cm and in width from 1 to 3 cm, offering wide scope for selection. Date palm trees are very productive and the fruit yield may be as high as 100-200 kg per tree.

Of the estimated 105 million date palms in the world, over two-thirds are in Arab countries. Approximately 600 different kinds of dates are available in the Arab countries, accounting for 60% of the world's production. In Iraq, there are presently around 450 female cultivars.

Some of the desirable characters in the date palm include: glossy black fruit (cv. Abbada), late maturity (cv. Barhee), firm texture (cvs. Bedraya, Thoory, Horra), moisture tolerance (cvs. Dayri, and Halawy), superior quality (cvs. Amir Hajj), and long fruitstalk (cvs. Horra, Kush Zebda). Dry or soft dates are eaten out-of-hand, or may be seeded and stuffed, or chopped and used in a great variety of ways: on cereal, in pudding, bread, cookies, ice cream, or candy bars. The fruit is a high energy food of high sugar content, as well as a good source of iron and potassium.

Surplus dates are made into cubes, paste, spread, powder (date sugar), jam, jelly, juice, syrup or vinegar. Cull fruits are dehydrated, ground and mixed with grain to form a very nutritious stockfeed. Dried dates are fed to camels and horses. Young leaves are cooked and eaten as vegetable. The seeds are soaked in water until soft and then fed to horses, cattle, camels, sheep and goats. Dried and ground up, they are now included in chicken feed. The seed contains 6-8% of a yellow-green, non-drying oil suitable for use in soap and cosmetic products. In addition, the seeds may be processed chemically as a source of oxalic acid and are burned to make charcoal for silversmiths, and they are often strung in necklaces and beads.

Threats to ~20 million date palms in Iraq have been highlighted recently in a number of reports. The Red Palm Weevil is threatening the country's date industry and the very survival of the date palm trees. The pest was first known in India some 110 years ago; however, it wasn't until 1918 that the weevil presented a serious threat to the date palm industry in Iraq. Unfortunately, the only effective control measure is to cut down the infected trees and destroy them at an early stage to prevent the weevil from spreading over large areas. On the other hand, drought, due to a lengthy rainless period and drying up of many water wells, and, as a consequence, increased water and soil salinity, are two serious threats to the expanding date palm plantations in Iraq, in particular, and in some other parts of Arabia in general.

Constraints to date palm production in Iraq include: drought, high salinity, aged trees, diseases, and genetic erosion. Date palm groves in Iraq are aging; almost one-third of productive date palm trees are beyond the limits of their productive years.

Economic and social factors have decreased the diversity of date palm groves in Iraq and the composition of these groves as to the number of varieties witnessed a sharp decline in the recent years.

An ecogeographical and socioeconomic survey is necessary to collect all available information on date palm in Iraq, including indigenous knowledge. This will precede the establishment of a database and a field genebank for the most important varieties. Moreover, it is necessary to screen available germplasm for salinity tolerance at different developmental stages, and to survey the most important pests and diseases affecting the date palm in the country. This effort should lead to building a database on available date palm cultivars and their horticultural characteristics and distribution.

7.7. Medicinal plants

More than 400 species of medicinal plants have been identified in Iraq. These are either herbs, shrubs, or trees. The importance of these plants as sources of medicinal products has been recognized by local people since times immemorial. Some of these plants are being cultivated and marketed by farm families.

Iraq harbors ~ 400 medicinal plant species; they are being exploited in folk medicine; their conservation is urgent.

These plants are massively used by Bedouins or local people in folk medicine, either as hot or cold drinks; or chewed as raw, fresh or dried plant parts. Also, some medicinal plants, or their products, are being used externally to cure dermal diseases, insect or animal bites, and sometimes for the treatment of hair problems.

Information about the medicinal and aromatic plants of Iraq is scattered in a range of different works; however, women farmers harbor tremendous indigenous knowledge of these plants and their uses.

An ethnobotanical survey, carried out in central Iraq, identified 97 medicinal plant species belonging to 43 plant families. Most of these plants are endangered and over-exploited. The threat imposed by collecting them from the wild for domestic use and by overgrazing is enormous.

Some medicinal plants in Iraq: *Abutilon pannosum, A. muticum, A. glaucum, Adonis aestvalis, Alhagi mourorum, Ammi visnaga, Anemone coronarcium, Androcymbium gramineum, Asphodelus microcarpus, Atropa belladonna, Azadarachta indica, Brassica alba, Brassica campestris, Brassica nigra, Bryonia cretca, Calendula officinalis, Calotropis procera, Capparis spinosa, Centaurea phyllocephala, Cleome quinquenervia, Colchicum spp. Corcus spp., Echium italicum, Ephedra foliate, Echium vulgare, Fagonia bruguieri, Ferula assa-foetida, Grylycyrrhiza glabra, Haloxylon articulatum, Humuls lupulus, Jasminum grandiflorum, Lepidium sativum, Marrubium vulgare, Peganum harmala, Pelorgonium odoratissimum, Pimpinella anisum, Plantago ovata Portulaca oleracea, Prosopis fracta, Quercus infectoria, Salvia aegyptiaca, Salvia spinosa, Solanum nigrum, Sonchus oleraceus, Teucrium polium, Thymus capitatus, Verbena officinalis*

7.8. Crop Protection

There are no exact data on crop losses caused by plant pests and diseases of Iraq's major field crops, fruit trees and vegetables. However, according to an Iraqi Agriculture Ministry report, in 1999, agricultural diseases infected 50-80 percent of Iraq's agricultural crops and fruits.

Weeds infested the date palm fields and are harboring insects/pests such as Humaira and Dubas. This is adversely affecting the production of dates. Early in 1998, a build-up of both the Humaira and Dubas insects in palm trees was noticed in the southern parts of Iraq. A campaign to control these two pests, covering some 40,175 ha of date palm plantations in six Iraqi governorates, resulted in increased date yields. On the other hand, in 1999, some 97,500 ha of cereals and more than 36,000 ha of date plantation were sprayed. A second spraying campaign, carried out in May and June 1997, resulted in yield increases of wheat and dates estimated to be worth about US$35 million.

The major insects and diseases attacking wheat and barley in Iraq are as follows.

Insects: Sunn pest (*Eurygaster integriceps* Put.) was first detected in Iraq at the beginning of 21st century, it causes severe damage to wheat and barley and is found in the most important wheat-producing areas of Iraq. It is Iraq's most important insect pest of wheat and barley causing severe damage to these crops. Sunn pest was found mainly in northern Iraq, especially in areas with consistent rainfall, and also at low densities in irrigated areas. Natural enemies, including predators, parasitoids, fungi and bacteria, are being considered in an integrated program for sunn pest management.

Crop protection measures are mostly ineffective because of lack of chemicals, equipment and trained personnel.

Less important cereal pests include *Dolycoris baccarum* L., *Aelia acuminata* L., *Syringopais temperatella* Led., *Carpocoris podicus, Cephus pygmaeus* L., *Oria musculosa* Hubn., *Exaeretopus tritici* Williams and *Zabrus mono* Menetries.

Plant diseases of wheat include: covered smut, *Tilletia foetida;* stem rust, *Puccinia graminis tritici;* and ergot, *Clavicepts jourpura.* Plant diseases of barley include: loose smut, *Ustilago hordei* and black stem rust, *Puccinia graminis hordei.* The ear cockle nematode, *Anguinis tritici,* is found on both wheat and barley.

7.9. Seed Industry

Iraqi cereal production dropped sharply in the past decade due to problems with its seed multiplication system, leading to degradation of seed quality and productivity. Planting low-quality seeds during the 1980s and 1990s led to problems of weed and pest infestation, low productivity and an inability to use seed-processing machinery efficiently. Lack of high-yielding seed has reduced farm efficiency and often forced poor farmers to abandon their lands.

The seed industry in Iraq suffered major setbacks in the pas 20 years.

FAO implemented a project to equip laboratories for seed testing and to train technicians on field inspection and seed certification.

To help Iraq improve seed quality, UNDP launched an initiative in 1998 at the request of the government to restore the seed multiplication program. The U.N. Food and Agriculture Organization (FAO) is implementing the US$1 million project, building up stocks of healthy, genetically pure seeds for multiplication, based on modern agricultural standards.

Initially, the project imported 45 metric tons of wheat seed, which was distributed to selected farmers for multiplication. In 2001, 5,000 metric tons of high-quality seed replaced low-yielding wheat varieties with new, more productive ones. The project's goal was to produce enough certified seed to meet 70 percent of the country's requirements within five years and eventually enable Iraq to meet all its cereal needs.

The project also helped upgrade technical skills at Iraq's State Board of Seed Testing and Certification and agricultural research centers. It has trained technical personnel at five State Board laboratories across the country. The State Board is responsible for quality control of all seed production.

The project has also trained laboratory technologists and field inspectors at the agricultural research centers in variety maintenance, seed testing, seed health testing, variety identification, field crop certification, vegetable seed certification and field inspection.

Detailed information on seed production in Iraq is lacking. One exception, however, is information on seed sources and varieties of potato which are being imported mainly from the Netherlands through a privately-operated potato project in Iraq.

The most widespread variety is Bintje. Although outyielded in field trials and prone to sprouting and secondary growth in the spring planting, Bintje is preferred by consumers for its taste and texture. Varieties under evaluation include Radosa, Desiree, Amigo, Marijke, Estima, Jaerla, Ostara, and Wilja. Ten to fourteen thousand tons of seed are presently imported for the spring crop from the Netherlands.

Storage is very serious constraint to potato production in Iraq. At present the only seed source for the fall crop is the spring harvest. Seed tubers must be stored for 65-90 days. Only limited cold storage facilities are available, at a cost of about US$160 to keep a ton of potatoes for three months. Farmers without access to cold stores must utilize basements and other makeshift arrangements with or without ventilation. In the northern hills dark, insulated mud and straw huts are traditionally used for storing potatoes

8. Forest Resources

8.1. Natural Forests

The highest ridges of the Zagros Mountains contain Iraq's only forests, some of them quite extensive, preserved by the isolation and ruggedness of the area. Most of the mountain slopes permit only grazing; lower and more gentle slopes support fruit and nut trees.

Historically, deforestation and over-grazing in the Armenian highlands (eastern Turkey) is believed to be the source of the silt load that is considered to be the root cause of the decline of the Mesopotamian civilization and the irrigation system on which it depended.

The main value of these forests is for the fuel they can produce. Iraq's forests have undergone heavy cutting in recent years to supply charcoal and firewood to urban markets. It is estimated that the total yield from the country's forests annually is about 10,000 tons of charcoal and 20,000 tons of wood fuel, involving the felling of about 2,000 hectares of mature forest every year, according to FAO figures. Secondary forest products include gallnuts, harvested in considerable quantity for leather tanning, and gum.

Iraq's forests are threatened by cutting and uprooting.

Few areas in Iraq now have woodlands as well developed as those in North America or even in nearby Turkey. However, historical evidence indicates that forests once clothed slopes that are now almost bare or ragged. Reforestation and afforestation programs during the last ~ 40 years demonstrated that many previously treeless habitats can, given proper care, produce impressive forests of selected species.

The indigenous mountain forests of Iraq have been mapped and divided into broad categories based on the quality and density of the stocking. Of the 1,700,000 hectares of forestry, about 900,000 hectares consist of exploitable oak forest. At higher elevations are alpine plants that can survive harsh weather, and open parkland.

The Forest Service has started several forest developmental schemes in the mountain forests. Most of these have the dual objective of reducing erosion and flash runoff and of enriching the oak forest by the introduction of coniferous species (mostly *Pinus brutia, Cupressus sempervirens* and *C. arizonica*).

Seedlings of these species require watering for the first two or three summers, after which they become established and survive on winter rainfall. Watering is both difficult and costly, which rather limits the scope of the work; nevertheless, a number of promising small plantations have been already established in the mountains.

In the Zagros mountains, over cutting and overgrazing have reduced some of Iraq's oak forests to scrubland. Stands of other trees - maple, hawthorn, and pistachio, for example - remain, however. Release from grazing alone is sufficient to secure a very marked improvement in erosion control, and since the forests are all more or less heavily grazed, it would seem that the improved management of forest range is likely to become the most important aspect of future forest policy in the mountain catchments.

Regulating the cutting of forests for fuel and charcoal still remains a problem. The charcoal trade, with its urban centers in the lowlands, has been prohibited altogether recently, though the Forest Service still cannot prevent entirely the flow of contraband charcoal; there is little doubt that a considerable reduction in charcoal consumption has ensued.

More attention is being given to problems of watershed management, especially in the catchments of the huge new flood storage reservoirs planned or under construction in the mountains.

8.2.   Afforestation and Reforestation

The Forest Service, as a part of its afforestation efforts, established new plantations in the treeless lowlands, the first step in a long-term policy designed to make Iraq near self-sufficient in wood products. Many exotic species have been introduced, among them *Eucalypts* and hybrid *Poplar* and subtropical pines of the Mexican group, although indigenous species - notably the black poplar and the eastern plane - as well as long-established exotics such as the *Casuarina* spp. or *Eucalypts camaldulensis* and *E. microtheca,* form the bulk of these plantations.

Under the hot, desert climate of Iraq, water for irrigation is applied on a lavish scale, usually by pump lift from rivers and canals, and applications totaling 1,000 to 1,500 millimeters a year are not unusual. The land available, though sometimes troubled with salinity, is usually of good agricultural quality, and tree growth on these rich sites with abundant water and plenty of sunshine is phenomenally rapid. Poplars and eucalypts grow in height from 4 to 6 meters a year and in some of the earlier pioneer plantations - none more than ten years old - many of the trees are already large enough to yield telephone poles or small sawlogs. Mean annual increment rates of 20 cubic meters per hectare are expected and, if plans for establishing 20,000 hectares of plantations in the next two decades go through, Iraq should be self-sufficient in wood.

In the 75,000-hectare Musayib Canal Project, for example, the Forest Service planned for windbreaks to be planted along the banks of all main and lateral canals and drains. These plantations are expected to serve as a demonstration and to give the initiative to settlers to plant tree rows and farm wood-lots in their own holdings. In fact, extensive and systematic windbreak planting is expected to have far-reaching effects on crop yields and may also lead to considerable savings in the use of irrigation water as a result of lowered evapo-transpiration rates. Such plantations can be used for experimental purposes, especially under the extreme climatic conditions of lower Mesopotamia.

8.3. Fuelwood and Wood Needs:

Average annual consumption per inhabitant may vary from 0.02 to more than 1 m³ of air-dried fuelwood. The proportion of wood fuels increases with the altitude, both because wood is more abundant in mountainous areas than in the lowlands, at least up to about 1,000 m, and because family incomes are lower.

In certain mountainous zones fuelwood requirements are undoubtedly much higher; this is the case in the massifs of North Africa, Iraq and Turkey, where fuelwood requirements are at least 1.5 m³/person/year.

Information about the wood cover are often erroneous or incomplete. Nevertheless, an attempt has been made to give an estimate of the wood cover, distinguishing between:

(a) Natural forests, and

(b) Forest plantations, row plantations, farm woodlots and fruit-tree plantations (vines, olives).

It is evident that natural forest formations constitute a limited source (about one-third) of supply of fuelwood in Iraq. The annual fuelwood supply derived from forest plantations is estimated at about 108 million m³/yr, whereas other woody resources contribute 300 million m³/year. Naturally, the share of rural population of woody resources utilizable as fuelwood is almost double the share of urban population, i.e., 0.235 vs. 0.124 m³/year.

Overall needs of fuelwood in Iraq in 1980 were estimated at about 0.6 m³/year/person, and the total deficit was estimated at about 2,445,000 m³/year. However, by 2000, the total needs of the rural population were projected to be 6,000,000 m³/year.

Although Iraq, at one time, had ambitious forest plantation programs, the last two decades have shown that there is often a time lag between the establishment of programs and their effective implementation. The estimated area that was planned for establishment between 1980 and 2000 and its output were 80,000 ha and 640,000 m³/year, respectively.

9. Rangelands

9.1. Rangeland Management and Rehabilitation

Rangeland or steppe, which provides essential feed resources for sheep and goats make up about 50% of the total area of Iraq; however, this vital resource is being damaged at a catastrophic rate, not only by desertification, but also by over-exploitation to supply urban centers with animal products. Moreover, the vegetative cover is being exploited as a source of fuelwood. Research on fuelwood gathering in Iraq in the late 1960s suggested that a nomad tent of 10 persons would consume 3.5-4 tons of dry wood a year of the contemporary above-ground biomass in the rangelands of 200-500 kg per hectare.

-Rangelands and steppe make up ~50% of land area in Iraq.

-Permanent pastures make up ~9.0% of Iraq's land area.

-Overgrazing and uprooting of range shrubs caused a decline in range productivity, soil erosion and environmental degradation.

Overgrazing is an important part of the degradation process of Iraqi rangelands; however, opportunistic barley cultivation in the steppe and semi-desert in years of above average rainfall, contributed to the process. Four decades ago, the rangelands of Iraq supplied 60-80% of the small ruminants' diet; at present, however, they can barely meet 5-10% of these requirements.

Rangelands of Iraq are resources that require the most collective action in their management. The wide areas they cover and the poverty of the people living in these areas have always pushed successive Iraqi governments to consider rangeland development as their main turf because pastoral communities were perceived as lacking the financial, technical and institutional capacity to control and manage rangeland resources.

The land appropriation policy followed by successive Iraqi governments was supported by the assumption that the government, with its technical institutions, was better equipped both financially and technically to manage and improve the productivity of rangeland resources. This appropriation was also complemented with the reorganization of the local communities into cooperatives, settlement and involvement in agricultural production.

Fig. 11. Rangeland area in Iraq during the period 1960-2000.

State appropriation, which led to the transfer of the managerial roles of rangeland from traditional tribal institutions to government institutions, did not preclude communities from continuing to informally manage the resources even though they did not have legal rights over the use of the resource base. This contradiction created a situation of confusion that prevented tribal groups from better managing their pastoral resources and fostered illegal appropriation of rangelands and led to disputes.

9.2. Rangeland Problems

Rangelands in Iraq continue to face three important issues. The first issue relates to the need for a policy framework that would improve the performance of the livestock sector. The second concerns the legal frame work that would support collective action and foster community and individual stewardship for better management of rangeland resources. The third expresses the needs to transform or improve existing institutions to match the needs for technical innovations that would improve the efficiency of livestock production systems.

In the low rainfall areas of Iraq, small ruminants (sheep and goats) represent the principal economic output and contribute a large proportion of the income of farmers and nomadic or semi-nomadic herders. The country has experienced substantial increases and decreases in animal numbers over the last four decades. Prior to 1990, livestock producers were encouraged to increase flock sizes by the increased demand for animal products combined with favorable price ratios between livestock products and barley, the principal livestock feed; feed subsidies and other measures intended to mitigate the effects of feed shortages, especially in drought years have provided further incentives to retain greater numbers of animals.

Expansion in flock size and flock numbers has been particularly noticeable in rangelands, where more native pastures are open to free grazing. A generation ago, the native pasture vegetation in these rangelands provided a large proportion of the feed needs of the small ruminant population. Today, however, the natural rangelands can no longer provide such a high component of animal feed needs. As livestock numbers have grown, so has supplemental feeding, mainly of barley grain, straw, and industrial crop by-products (feed blocks have been recently introduced). The contribution of natural grazing as a proportion of total feed resources in Iraq has declined from around 70% in the 1950s to only 10-25% at present. Not only are rangeland resources insufficient to meet current demand, the absolute level of this feed source is falling due to overgrazing, removal of vegetation through plowing or for fuel wood, and soil erosion. The decreasing contribution of rangelands in sheep diets has resulted in heightened concerns about the needs to improve and conserve rangeland resources.

Unfortunately, institutional reforms have, in most cases, eroded the capacity and strength of traditional pastoral institutions. Such a situation precluded the Iraqi Bedouins from taking over the roles that are being sought for them both in terms of rangeland conservation as well as improvement.

Though, Iraq, for many decades, has been exploring new ways to further enhance the decision-making environment under which pastoral communities and their local institutions make their production decisions, the main challenge of this process has been striking the right balance between the rights and roles of traditional pastoral communities and those of the state and its institutions. The perceived difficulty of defining the roles and rights of pastoral communities is generally based on the nature of the extensive production system and the multitude of rules and conventions governing resource access and use. As such, there have been very little attempts during the past forty years, during which the state was undertaking most of the agricultural policies including rangelands, to integrate customary institutional frameworks and range management practices in policy formulation.

Inadequate and poor quality feed sources (especially during the dry season) is the most serious constraint to sheep production in Iraq. The prospects for the future are not encouraging. According to a recent study by the International Centre for Agricultural Research in the Dry Areas (ICARDA), the projected feed deficit in Iraq is expected to double every ten years (years 1992, 2000 and 2010) in response to the increase in livestock population. With the encroachment of cropping in the grazing areas and disappearance of dry season grazing reserves, sheep production has become very dependent on the availability of crop residues and by-products and purchased feed, especially during mating and early pregnancy (June - September). In most parts of Iraq, it has become necessary to all producers (large or smallholder) to access supplemental feeds (barley, wheat bran, straw and crop residues) or to abandon sheep production. For example, the smallholders are forced to purchase up to 50% - 70% of the feed needed. The small herders face difficulties of raising sheep if the cereal crop fails due to drought.

Rangeland degradation is the most extensive among the three major land uses in Iraq, i.e., irrigated farming, dryland farming and grazing. It is estimated that more than 70% of Iraq's pastoral lands are degraded. Overgrazing by livestock is the principal land problem, coupled with cutting of woody species as a fuel source. This high percentage of the country's rangeland that suffers from overuse stems from the extensive, low intensity character of pastoral land use, the slow response to land management changes in arid climates, and the social and economic problems associated with reducing livestock numbers on heavily used rangelands.

9.3. Alternative Feed Sources

One of the main limiting factors affecting sheep production in Iraq is the shortage of feed resources, especially protein. Cereal stubble grazing and hand-feeding of chopped straw are the main components of the sheep diet for a considerable part of the year.

Inadequate and poor quality feed sources are the most serious constraints to sheep production and productivity in Iraq.

Research conducted in Iraq on feed blocks indicates that this technology offers various options to sheep owners in the nutritional management of their flocks. The feed block technology is simple and does not require sophisticated equipment. Manufacturing and handling of feed blocks is also easy and can be done at the farm level using the family labor.

Multi-nutrient feed blocks were manufactured from urea and locally available agro-industrial by-products. The feed blocks may be made using different formulas with different levels of urea, binders and a wide range of agro-industrial by-products available locally. For instance, in Iraq, date pulp, rice bran, poultry waste are the main agro-by-products.

Sheep in the semi-arid areas of Iraq are heavily dependent on cereal stubble grazing as their sole source of feed during summer, which coincides with the mating season resulting in lower productivity of the flock. Results of research showed that under such situations feed blocks, used as a supplementary feed, resulted in considerable improvement in ewes' weight gain, conception, lambing and twinning rates.

Multi-nutrient feed blocks are improving livestock production and productivity in Iraq.

Hand feeding during winter (November to January) is frequently practiced because of shortage of grazing and green roughage. During this period the sheep mostly depend on whole barley grain and stored straw. The introduction and use of feed blocks containing high energy ingredients, as supplementary feed, has resulted in a significant replacement of barley grain and minimized the use of roughage and concentrates.

Furthermore, it was demonstrated in Iraq that adding cotton seed meal can enrich feed blocks and improve their nutritional value. Results show that when cotton seed meal (as source of protein) and vitamins A, D, and E are added to the basic formulae of feed blocks, considerable improvement in ewes' conception rate, lambing percentage and twinning percentage can be achieved.

The effect of feed blocks supplement on reproductive performance of Awassi ewes (On-station, Mosul) can be illustrated by the following figures. Control ewes lost 35 g/day as compared to a gain of 5 g/day for those fed on feed blocks. More importantly the conception and lambing rates of control and feed block-fed ewes were 89, 115 and 78 and 115%, respectively. Moreover, feeding Awassi ewes high energy feed blocks, during the hand-feeding period, resulted in 59% more milk production at 62% of the cost as compared to ewes fed the traditional way.

10. Livestock

10.1. Livestock Production and Management

Iraq's rich and distinctive livestock population is largely a result of being in the center of origin from which the most common farm animal species came. However, productivity and feeding conditions of these animals, naturally limited by the land's pasture potential, are not optimum.

Ancient traditions in rural communities that are significantly involved in animal husbandry still survive and maintain the diversity of Iraqi cattle, sheep, goats and buffalos. However, in some cases these practices have been greatly modified, especially after the massive import and dissemination of foreign livestock and the extensive crossing with local breeds.

Livestock and poultry production is limited by feed shortages, and lack of veterinary services

Livestock contributed about one-third of Iraqi rural families' income prior to the 1960s. In the past, a substantial part of the rural population had been nomadic, moving animals between seasonal grazing areas. Sheep and goats were the most important livestock, supplying meat, wool, milk, skins, and hair. A 1978 government survey estimated the sheep population at 9.7 million and the goat population at 2.1 million. Sheep and goats were tended primarily by nomadic and semi-nomadic groups. The 1978 survey estimated the number of cattle at 1.7 million, the number of water buffalo at 170,000, the number of horses at 53,000, and the number of camels at 70,000.

According to 1990 statistics, there were 1,500,000 cattle, 8,300,000 sheep, 2,350,000 goats, and 145,000 buffaloes in Iraq; however, the animal population in Iraq has declined dramatically since 1990. Between 1990 and 1995, the number of cows declined by 34 per cent, the number of buffaloes by 46 per cent, the number of sheep by 42 per cent, and the number of goats by 81 per cent.

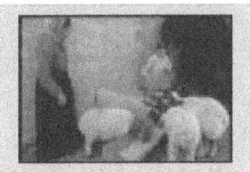

In the 1970s, the government started to emphasize livestock and fish production, in an effort to add protein to the national diet. But 1985's red meat production (about 93,000 tons) and milk production (375,000 tons) were, respectively, about 24 and 23 percent less than the 1975 figures. Total production of processed chicken and fish almost doubled, to about 20,000 tons apiece, from 1981 to 1985, while egg production increased substantially, to more than 1 billion per year. Iraq nevertheless continued to import substantial quantities of frozen poultry, meat, and fish to meet local needs for protein.

Traditionally, Iraqi people have depended heavily on meat and other livestock based products in their regular diet. However, critical shortages of animal products, after 1990, reduced the country's capability to produce enough animal products and caused their prices to increase beyond the purchasing power of the majority of the Iraqi people.

The latest statistics (2001) showed that food consumption by the Iraqi population in 1997 was a small fraction of what it was in 1990. The production of milk and milk products have virtually collapsed due to poor health of dairy cows and lack of equipment.

Consumption of animal products/ person, kg/year (1990 & 1997):

Milk 15 – 3
Red meat 13 – 2
Poultry 125 – 1.5
Fish 3.5 – 1.0

The main factors limiting livestock and poultry production include critical shortages of feed, veterinary services and drugs, machinery and equipment and lack of spare parts. Another constraint, of growing importance, is the gradual shift in land use of pasture land for opportunistic grain production.

Poultry consumption in Iraq was high because of increased individual income before 1990. This caused an increase in imported poultry and generated the need for a transport and storage system for perishable products. For these reasons, the government initiated a scheme to establish and develop large poultry projects to supply the country with sufficient poultry and poultry products.

During the 1980s, there were 8,353 small and 25 large poultry projects, which provided about 1,688 million eggs, 106 million hatching eggs, and 250,000 tons of chicken meat, annually. However, many of these projects are either closed down or are functioning at a fraction of full capacity.

10.2. Animal Health

The animal disease situation in Iraq has been aggravated by the collapse of the veterinary infrastructure and disease investigation, surveillance and diagnostic services in the country. The government has been unable to adequately monitor and control the spread of these diseases, partly because of the difficulties it has in obtaining equipment and supplies, particularly vaccines. Foot-and-mouth disease, for example, has long been a major constraint to intensive livestock production in Iraq, and in spite of vaccinations—twice or even three times a year—the disease has caused serious economic losses in some of the large dairy herds in the country.

Generally poor access to veterinary service, high cost of drugs and vaccines, lack of skills, knowledge or interest in disease surveillance and reporting, and the absence of trained auxiliaries limit livestock production. However, disease constraints are more pronounced.

Animal diseases are on the rise due to the collapse of the veterinary infrastructure.

Poor interaction between researchers, farmers, extension workers and policy makers is a major obstacle to improved sheep productivity in Iraq. Most of the research results are not suitable for adoption by the sheep producers because experiments are usually designed and developed under the controlled environments of the experimental stations, and because the problems researched do not reflect those facing the small sheep herders. In addition, lack of economic incentives caused by unfavorable price policies, poor marketing infrastructure and lack of financial resources are some of the major obstacles to improved sheep production. Normally farmers do not accept innovations which require additional activities beyond household labor capacity or beyond their financial resources.

11. Fisheries and Aquaculture

The fish and aquaculture production sector employed some 25,000 people, and the production for 1997 was about 35,200 tons, and the average per capita supply was 1.6 kg/year. Annual production for the period 1991-1997 was 31,000 tone and the estimated production in 1998 dropped down to 13,400 tons.

Iraq has a limited coastal area. There is a marine fishing cooperative in Basra, which is active in Iraqi territorial waters and the Persian Gulf. Fish technology is not highly developed in Iraq. The General Institute of Fish Technology is the official organization responsible for management and utilization of fish resources in the country.

Marine resources in Iraq include:
-River fish,
-Marine fish,
-Shrimp.

Marine resources in Iraq include river fish, marine fish, and shrimp. Fish production has been seriously affected after 1990. The only central facility for rearing and supplying fish fingerlings to fish farmers and to rivers, ponds, lakes and dams to renew and maintain the fish population in the country is now functioning only at half capacity. The seasonal capacity of this fish hatchery was 50 million; however, due to the deteriorating conditions of its machinery, equipment, including laboratory chemicals and feed and hormone supplies, its performance has drastically declined.

The inland fisheries are based in great part on *Cyprinus* spp., while the most important Iraqi indigenous fishes belong to the genus *Barbus*. Table x. presents the most important fish species in Iraq.

The total aquaculture area in production in 1998 was estimated at 7,500 ha. The main species produced are common carp and, to a lesser extent, grass and silver carp.

A total of 1,893 fish farms are licensed for aquaculture, with an average area of 4 ha. Very few (10 farms) are larger than 100 ha. The government planned to construct a US$160 million deep-sea fishing facility in Basra and predicted that, within 10 years, freshwater fishing would supply up to 100,000 tons of fish

Research and development in fisheries and aquaculture are carried out by a number of specialized research center, along with some colleges of agriculture and veterinary medicine, these include: The Fish research Center at Zafarniah near Baghdad; The Marine Science Center, Basra; IPA Agricultural Research Center in

Baghdad; The Central hatchery at Swairah; and The Agricultural Institute at Musayib in southern Iraq.

Marine fish in Iraq include: *Tenualosa ilisha* (River Shad) *Liza oligolepis* (Mullet) *Pampus argenteus* (Silver Pomfret) *Arius thalassinus* (Catfish) *Acanthocybium solandri* (Wahoo); inland freshwater fish include: *Cyprinus sharpey* (Binni), *Barbus xanthopterus* (Kattan), *Barbus grypus* (Shabbout), *Liza abu* (Khshni), *Silurus triostegus* (Djirri), *Barbus luteus* (Himri), *Asalus eorase* (Shilik), *Cyprinus carpio* (Common Carp); and aquaculture fish include: *Cyprinus carpio* (Common Carp), *Hypophthalmichthys molitrix* (Silver Carp), *Ctenopharyngodon idellus* (Grass Carp)

12. Apiculture

The indigenous honeybee in Iraq is *Apis mellifera syriaca*. A species reported to be *Apis florea* has been documented in eastern Iraq although it is not known whether this species has naturally increased its distribution westwards from Asia, or this represents an introduction by man. According to the Arab Organization for Agricultural Development, the production of honey in Iraq in 1997 was 125 tons, and the number of beekeepers was 17,000.

Bees' contribution to food production and nutrition, both by pollinating food crops and by producing honey, can be demonstrated in the 500,000 traditional hives in Iraq during the 1980s. However, during 1985-1987 a worldwide devastating pest, the Asian predatory mite (*Varroa jacobsoni*), caused a sharp decline in the number of hives and the health of the remaining ones.

A thriving apiculture of 500,000 hives before 1980 was reduced to ~ 500 in 1991.

Recently, FAO revived the industry by restoring ~ 30,000 hives.

The Iraqi Beekeepers' Association estimates that 90 percent of the over 500,000 honeybee hives in Iraq had been lost to *Varroa jacobsoni* by 1987, and that by 1991, a mere 500 hives remained. In response, FAO and the UN Department of Humanitarian Affairs funded the US$200,000 Emergency Assistance Project to Restore Honeybee Populations for Crop Pollination and Honey Production in Iraq. The project aims to help beekeepers establish sustainable beekeeping techniques and adequate hygiene practices.

Although it is difficult to quantify the reduction in crop pollination by bees in Iraq, poorly formed fruit is on sale in local markets, a typical sign of inadequate pollination. In Mosul, people have been employed to pollinate gourd crops manually, as farmers have realized that natural pollination is inadequate.

The most recent threat to Iraq's honeybee population is the so-called "crawling disease". First reported in early 1994, one year later the disease had already considerably reduced the 30,000 bee hives re-established under the project. Believed to be caused by secondary viral or other infections, crawling disease causes severe weakening of the bees and loss of honey production.

13. The National Agricultural Research System

13.1. Historical background

In the 1920s, a "Directorate General of Agriculture", affiliated with the Ministry of Economics and Transport, started agricultural research activities and established the first experimental stations at Abu Ghraib, near Baghdad and Neinevah, near Mosul, and the Central Veterinary Laboratory, which focused its work on the diagnosis and control of pests and animal diseases.

Agricultural research in Iraq started in the 1920s and underwent major re-structuring ever since.

In the 1940s, agricultural research activities were administered by the Directorate General for Agricultural Research and Extension (DGARE) of the Ministry of Agriculture (MOA), with its headquarters at Abu Ghraib, near Baghdad. A College of Agriculture, and a College of Veterinary Medicine, affiliated with the University of Baghdad, were established in 1952 and 1956, respectively.

In 1958, the Directorate General for Agricultural Research and Projects (DGAREJ) was established as the only governmental body responsible for agricultural research in the country, except for research on agroforestry, which was assigned to the State Board of Forestry. In 1968, however, DGAREJ was terminated and agricultural research activities were assigned to different departments responsible for agronomic, horticultural, plant protection, extension, and animal resources research. During the 1970s, agricultural research witnessed a revival and was expanded as more and more research stations and centers were established in different parts of the country.

During the 1960s, a College of Agriculture and a College of Veterinary Medicine were established at Mosul University in 1964 and 1968, respectively. Another college of agriculture was established at the University of Basra in 1873, and the Agricultural and Biological Center of the Iraqi Atomic Energy Commission, was established in 1967. Recently, this center was sub-divided into the following four centers: Agricultural Research Center, Fisheries Research Center, Seed Technology Center, and Biotechnology Center.

In 1980, the Ministry of Agriculture established the State Board for Applied Agricultural Research (SBAAR) to be responsible for all its agricultural research activities. When the Ministries of Agriculture and Irrigation were merged in 1987, the Center for Water and Soil Resources was included under SBAAR, which was named as The State Board for Agricultural Research and Water Resources (SBARWR). However, in 1990, SBARWR was terminated and was replaced by the State Board for Agricultural Research (SBAR) and The Center for Water and Soil Resources (CWSR). By 1993, the Ministries of Agriculture and Irrigation were separated again, and as a consequence, SBAR was affiliated with the Ministry of Agriculture, while CWSR went under the Ministry of Irrigation.

Five more Colleges of Agriculture were established during the 1990s; these were Tikrit, Anbar, Qadisiah, Sulaymaniyah and Dohuk; the last two were established in the autonomous region of Kurdistan.

13.2. The Current National Agricultural Research System (NARS)

The Iraqi NARS is currently composed of three main types of institutions, these are:

1. Institutions mainly specialized in agricultural research: The State Board for Agricultural Research (SBAR), and the Center for Water and Soil Research (CWSR); these represent 32% of the Full Time Equivalent (FTE) in agricultural research;

    Currently, Iraqi NARS is composed of researchers at the Ministries of Agriculture & Irrigation, Colleges of Agriculture & Veterinary Medicine, and The Iraqi Atomic Energy Commission.

2. Colleges of Agriculture and Veterinary Medicine, under the Ministry of Higher education and Scientific Research, these represent 49% of FTE; and

3. Other scientific and technical institutions for which agricultural research is a secondary mandate, such as the Agricultural and Biological Research Center of the Iraqi Atomic Energy Commission, which represents 19% of FTE.

13.2.1. The State Board for Agricultural Research (SBAR)

SBAR is the largest NARS institution. Its main mandate is agricultural research along with soil analysis, seed production, extension and training. At present, SABR consists of six main agricultural divisions: agronomy, horticulture and forestry, date palm and tissue culture, soils, animal resources and plant protection.

SBAR currently has 638 national permanent full-time staff, 266 of whom there are 37 Ph. D, 54 M. Sc., and 175 B. Sc. graduates. These researchers work in 14 research stations which cover all agro-ecological zones in the country.

Research activities cover both crop and animal production, with emphasis on wheat, barley, rice and corn. Considerable efforts are being devoted to develop industrial (e.g., cotton and sunflower) and horticultural (dryland and irrigated fruits and vegetables) crops. Research on forestry, fisheries, agricultural machinery and agricultural economics received increasing attention, especially during the last decade.

13.2.2. Center for Water and Soil Research (CWSR)

The Center employs a total of 58 professionals of whom there are 9 Ph. D., 9 M. Sc., and 40 B. Sc. graduates.

Researchers at this center work on soil erosion, siltation, salinization, land reclamation, irrigation systems, drainage, water pollution, soil surveys and land management.

13.2.3. Colleges of Agriculture and Veterinary Medicine

Information on five of the colleges of agriculture and three colleges of veterinary medicine is available and is presented below. These colleges are supervised by their respective universities under the auspices of the Ministry of Higher Education and Scientific Research. They are:

> (a) College of Agriculture, University of Baghdad, with 507 academic staff members (188 Ph. D., 150 M. Sc., and 169 B. Sc.); College of Agriculture and Forestry, Mosul University, with 267 academic staff members (107 Ph. D., 124 M. Sc. and 36 B. Sc.); College of Agriculture, Basra University, with 189 academic staff members (44 Ph. D., 79 M. Sc., and 66 B. Sc.); College of Agriculture, Tikrit University with 51 academic staff members (18 Ph. D., 19 M. Sc., and 14 B. Sc.); and College of Agriculture, Anbar University, with 46 academic staff members (11 Ph. D., 23 M. Sc and 12 B. Sc.).
>
> (b) The College of Veterinary Medicine, Baghdad University, is the largest with 293 academic staff members (91 Ph. D., 104 M. Sc. and 98 B. Sc.),

followed by the second at Mosul University with 127 academic staff members (31 Ph. D., 54 M. Sc., and 42 B. Sc.), and the third at Qadisiah University with thirty academic staff members (3 Ph. D., 12 M. Sc., and 15 B. Sc).

Most resources available to academic staff are devoted to teaching and a very limited amount (10-20%) of their time is devoted to research. Research activities carried out by the academic staff, although limited, address specific agro-ecological problems. The College of Agriculture, Baghdad University, is mainly concerned with irrigated agriculture and horticulture; at Mosul University, research is being conducted on small grains, dryland crop production, forestry and wood technology; production practices, and land management of gypsiferous soils are of interest to faculty of Tikrit University, whereas date palm, horticultural, and fisheries research is being conducted by Basra University. All colleges of Agriculture and Veterinary Medicine carry out some research on animal husbandry and animal diseases.

The four centers under the Iraqi Atomic Energy Commission (i.e., Agricultural Research Center, Fisheries Research Center, Seed Technology Center, and Biotechnology Center) have 392 academic staff members (43 Ph. D., 84 M. Sc., and 265 B. Sc) working on agricultural problems in the agronomic, horticultural, livestock, fisheries, natural resources, seed technology and biotechnology fields.

13.3. Research Policy

In the present economic climate, and for the last two decades, agricultural research managers and researchers in Iraq are increasingly faced with the challenge of raising the efficiency of agricultural research to maximize the output of enhanced technologies to farmers. To make the right decisions, they must have good information about the research systems they manage. Therefore, a national strategy for agricultural research and transfer of technology was formulated and adopted in 1995. The objectives of that strategy were to achieve:

In 1995, a Research Policy was developed to bring together all those involved in agricultural research, coordinate their efforts and try to solve food production problems in Iraq.

1. Food self-sufficiency through the adoption of new and more productive technologies,

2. A long-term sustainable agricultural production system through sound management and development of available resources, especially, water and land resources, and

74

3. Social and economic equity between agricultural sector and other sectors of the national economy.

The national strategy identified a serious side effect of the deteriorating budget of many research and extension services in the last decade. There has been, for example, a severe reduction in access to scientific information as library funds – and hence subscriptions to scientific journals – have been reduced drastically.

The national strategy identified the major research themes and outlined the requirements for planning and conducting agricultural research at the country, and at eco-regional levels. Moreover, the strategy called for accountability in conducting agricultural research and for practical, sound means of assessing, demonstrating, and improving research organizations' performance and results. Some of the highlights of this strategy are presented below:

1. Research programs should be applied and/or adaptive in nature. They should (i) be multidisciplinary in their approach and represent a continuum from research to on-farm trials and demonstrations and transfer of technology to end users; (ii) include socioeconomic components to ensure economic relevance and acceptance of results and recommendations by potential users; and (iii) be oriented towards developing and adopting new technologies, management practices and policies which address the problems and needs of the agricultural sector.

2. Research programs should emphasize integrated production systems in the fields of rainfed agriculture, irrigated agriculture, pasture and rangelands, and livestock husbandry.

3. The strategy mandates all components of the national agricultural research system with applied research and technology transfer, and with the responsibility of coordinating and supporting national agricultural research programs. This approach may have a beneficial impact on research planning, priority setting and management of research programs; also, it may help researchers carry out their research on farmers' fields and expedite technology transfer and adoption, and

4. The strategy defined the roles of various components of the national agricultural research system in order to

achieve stronger integration and better complementarity, especially under the prevailing economic climate in Iraq.

13.4. Human Resources

The Iraqi NARS currently has about 2,100 scientific and technical staff; expressed as Full Time Equivalents (FTE), it adds up to 671 FTEs. The faculty and staff of Iraqi universities represent ~ 50% of the human resources. However, this number is insufficient to work on the highly diverse and compounded agricultural problems arising from ~20 years of insufficient funding and changing priorities.

Institution	FTE
Agriculture	266
Irrigation	58
U Baghdad	127
U Mosul	67
U Basra	73
U Tikrit	47
U Anbar	13
U Qadisiah	8
U Sulaymaniyah	7
U Dohuk	5

It is obvious that there is a need for highly qualified and well trained human resources in the agricultural research sector. However, agricultural extension services and vocational agricultural education are in need of major improvements.

The governmental investment in the extension services in Iraq is very weak, at best. Budget allocations for the extension services dropped from 10% of total agricultural budget in the 970-1975 period, to 3% in the 1975-1980 period and down to 2% in the 1980-1983 period. The relative and actual decline in the budget of extension services are indicators of the need for highly qualified and motivated extension personnel capable of planning, developing and carrying out extension services in Iraq's diverse socioeconomic and agro-ecological farming sector.

The number of extension workers in 1990 was less than 200; in ratio to the number of farmers, this meant that one extension worker was serving approximately 10,000 farmers. These extension workers have the responsibility of assisting farmers in adopting new technologies, identifying specific or regional agricultural problems, communicating recommendations as to management practices and adoption of new varieties, etc.

13.5. Financial and Physical Resources

Funding for agricultural research is mainly provided through government allocations for research centers affiliated with Ministries of Agriculture and Irrigation and for Colleges of Agriculture and Veterinary Medicine. Additional funds, although marginal, are being secured through research contracts with developmental organizations, the private sector or through sale of improved seed.

Actual funds for research comprise a small fraction of budgets allocated for these research institutions, with very limited allocations available for operational and capital expenses.

Physical resources are deteriorating due to inability of NARS to purchase necessary equipment or afford high expenditure. A large portion (70%) of the scientific staff, educated during the 1970s and 1980s, is underemployed or unemployed.

13.6. National and International Linkages

Up until recently, linkages between the NARS institutions and the different agencies involved in agricultural research and extension were weak; they were limited to participation in joint committees of different research programs. Agricultural research was mostly undertaken without an overall coordination or joint planning. Similarly, the linkages between the extension services, developmental organizations and farmers, on the one hand, and research institutions, on the other, were very sporadic and ineffective.

Scientific linkages between the Iraqi NARS and international research institutes are week

However, in 1995, a national strategy for agricultural research and technology transfer was adopted, and stronger linkages between different parts of the Iraqi NARS were developed. Researchers from the different institutions started participating in research planning and evaluation, holding joint field days, seminars, and writing joint publications.

Working relationships with farmers, the extension services, and developmental agencies were highly improved. Adaptive research, in farmers' fields, is being conducted not only by extension agents, but also by faculty members.

International linkages are very limited; however, a number of regional (Arab Center for the Studies of Arid Lands and Dry Areas, ACSAD), and international research centers (The International Center for Agricultural Research In Dry Areas, ICARDA) and organizations (Food and Agriculture Organization of the United Nations, FAO) are being involved in agricultural research and development in Iraq, especially during the last decade.

14. Research Needs and Priorities

14.1. Restructuring The National Agricultural Research System

Agricultural research currently makes a modest contribution to national goals in Iraq. This may reflect wartime attitudes towards information and openness, rather than the priorities or capacities of the different organizations involved in agricultural research. Indeed, many of the staff of the Iraqi NARS earned strong research degrees in different fields of the agricultural and veterinary sciences, however, the internal efficiency and external relevance of NARS, at the present, are inadequate. Therefore, it might be necessary to (1) develop institutional innovations independent of the existing research and extension system, (2) develop institutional innovations within the research and extension system, or (3) improve the functioning of the existing institutions with emphasis on accountability.

> *Iraqi NARS is making a modest contribution to national goals.*
>
> *A large portion (~70%) of the scientific staff educated in the 1970s and 1980s is under-employed or unemployed.*

A strong and productive agricultural research and extension system in Iraq requires:

1. A coherent research policy designed to meet national development goals;
2. An organization compatible with the objectives and functions the government assigns to research;
3. An integrated set of management processes allowing the system to effectively mobilize and use the required resources; and
4. The ability to communicate effectively with its clientele, its partners in the scientific community, and the country's policy makers.

14.2. Capacity Building

It is clear that solid data on many vital aspect of the society, in general, and on the agricultural sector, in particular, do not exist. Therefore the Iraqi government will need to be prepared to invest resources in building research capacity in a variety of fields.

The importance of research capacity building is now so widely recognized that there are a number of excellent models to consider, and a number of international research facilities capable of providing assistance to Iraq. Building research capacity is, however, a long-term and costly endeavor.

Iraq no longer has an extension corps in direct contact with its farmers. At a time when the farmers are expected to make their own decisions on what crops to plant, there is no direct link with them to either guide their decisions or understand the basis for the decisions they make. Field research is needed to understand the factors that affect the choices farmers make and the outcomes they achieve, the absorption of labor by agriculture and off-farm employment opportunities, agricultural credit and marketing problems, the availability of inputs, and land management and conservation practices.

There is one extension agent for each 10,000 farmers in Iraq

Extension services are no longer in contact with farmers.

Capacity building of agricultural research and strengthening of the national agricultural research system can be accelerated through open access of the Iraqi NARS to the regional and international research community.

Agricultural research managers in Iraq will need to become acquainted with various methods of organizing research programs, developing skills in research proposal development, familiarizing themselves with a wide range of research methodologies, and establishing links with sources of research expertise abroad.

14.3. Strengthening the Role of Iraqi Universities in Agricultural Research

The need to strengthen the role of universities in Iraq's NARS has two underlying assumptions. The first is that universities have an underutilized potential to contribute efficiently, effectively, and sustainably to national agricultural research. Second is that the mobilization of universities' research potential together with the strengthening of the linkages between universities and other components of the NARS will provide benefits to society.

Iraqi universities are teaching institutions. It is necessary to strengthen their role as research and development institutes.

Among the many questions to be answered to strengthen the role of Iraqi universities in agricultural research are:

1.   What is the potential of each university in terms of scale, scope, and nature in addressing national agricultural research and development issues?
2.   What are the actual agricultural research activities of each university?
3.   How effective, efficient, and sustainable is university research in addressing national agricultural research priorities?
4.   What factors influence the agricultural research agenda of each university? and,

5.   What could be alternative mechanisms and opportunities to improve the   contribution of each university to achieve the goals of the NARS?

Among the expected outcomes of this evaluation process are: a self-diagnostic tool that can be used by Iraq to evaluate the current contribution of its many universities to the NARS, and generic lessons and guidelines for strengthening research collaboration between universities and other NARS components.

A recent study revealed that the universities' lack of contribution to national agricultural research is due to one or more of the following:

1. Absence of an explicit mandate for national agricultural research,
2. Absence of research priorities related to national research needs,
3. Missing functions of planning, coordination, and evaluation of research at the   university,
4. Existing physical facilities that are not used for research,
5. Existing potential of human resources that is not used for research,
6. Lack of funding for university research,
7. Missing incentives for university staff to do research,
8. Its relations with external institutions—for example, developed-country   universities and international donors—which do not encourage or support development-oriented research, and
9. Absence of linkages with users and potential clients of research

The same study showed that the poor linkages between the Iraqi universities and other NARS components were due to the following:

1.   Missing national research policy,
2.   Differing research objectives,
3.   Differing research activities,
4.   Missing information on ongoing and proposed research,
5.   Differing organizational structure, especially with regard to planning, coordinating, and monitoring and evaluation,
6.   Differing qualifications of staff members (degree-level or specialization)
7.   Differing reward systems,

8. Their belonging to different ministries with different budgets, rules, regulations, and demands,

9. Traditional linkages with different institutions (with different objectives)

10. Missing formal linkages, and

11. Missing incentives for staff members to link (assumption that costs are higher than benefits).

14.4. Research Needs and Priorities in the Rainfed, Irrigated, and Rangeland Production Systems of Iraq

Farmers in Iraq are struggling to produce under poor environmental conditions with few tools for coping with drought, salinity, insects, weeds, and diseases, and shortages in inputs (fertilizers, improved seed, etc.), and lack of appropriate technologies and machinery.

Iraq, a nation heavily dependent on food imports, may have to spend 3-5% of its agricultural gross domestic product on agricultural research. Annual social rate of return may exceed 20%.

After almost one decade of stagnant agricultural research, farmers need help to reduce their risks, improve their productivity, and protect their natural resources. Yet the kind of agricultural research that will benefit these farmers is, as yet, severely under-funded. The gains to society and to farmers, however, are high. Social rates of return to most investments in agricultural research, in some developing countries, have exceeded 20 percent a year. For Iraq, this is a most worthwhile investment.

Increased funding for agricultural research is particularly critical in Iraq. Despite this nation's heavy dependence on food imports, the public expenditures on research generally total less than 0.5 percent of its agricultural gross domestic product. By comparison, industrialized countries spend 2 to 5 percent.

Besides the technological tools for producing more agricultural goods, Iraqi farmers also require sound and supportive public policies. Trade, macroeconomic and sectoral policies must not discriminate against agriculture and must favor poverty reduction and food security. Policies must also provide incentives for sustainable natural resource management, such as secure property rights for small farmers. Above all, farmers must participate in making decisions and implementing programs that affect their livelihood.

Research needs and priorities for Iraqi agriculture can be classified under the following major research themes:

14.4.1. Crop improvement and germplasm enhancement, with an overall objective of increased yield and stability through genetic and agronomic improvement of the major (wheat, barley) and minor (food legumes, forage legumes, etc.) crops in the rainfed and irrigated lands of Iraq.

14.4.2. Production systems management, with a farming systems perspective, to integrate crops and livestock production, and to properly manage soil and water resources for the purpose of optimizing crop and livestock production in rainfed and irrigated areas.

14.4.3. Rehabilitation and improved management of native pastures and rangelands in the dry areas, and improvement of natural and sawn pasture in rangelands and under irrigation, as sources for livestock feed, and

14.4.3. Natural resources management to promote efficient, integrated, and sustainable use of land, water and agro-biodiversity resources in different agro-ecological zones of Iraq.

www.ingramcontent.com/pod-product-compliance
Lightning Source LLC
Chambersburg PA
CBHW080834180526

45168CB00006B/2677